TOWARD A PHILOSOPHY OF THE ACT · · · · ·

UNIVERSITY OF TEXAS PRESS SLAVIC SERIES, NO. *10*

MICHAEL HOLQUIST

General Editor

M. M. BAKHTIN

TOWARD A
PHILOSOPHY
OF THE ACT

TRANSLATION AND NOTES BY
VADIM LIAPUNOV

EDITED BY
MICHAEL HOLQUIST & VADIM LIAPUNOV

UNIVERSITY OF TEXAS PRESS, AUSTIN · · · · · · · · · · · ·

First edition, 1993

Requests for permission to reproduce material from this work should be sent to
Permissions, University of Texas Press, Box 7819, Austin, TX 78713-7819.

∞ The paper used in this publication meets the minimum requirements of
American National Standard for Information Sciences—Permanence of Paper for
Printed Library Materials, ANSI Z39.48-1984.

LIBRARY OF CONGRESS CATALOGING-IN-PUBLICATION DATA

Bakhtin, M. M. (Mikhail Mikhaïlovich), 1895–1975.
    [K filosofii postupka. English]
    Toward a philosophy of the act / by M. M. Bakhtin ; translation and notes by
Vadim Liapunov ; edited by Vadim Liapunov and Michael Holquist. — 1st ed.
        p.   cm. — (University of Texas Press Slavic series ; no. 10)
    Includes bibliographical references and index.
    ISBN 0-292-76534-7. — ISBN 0-292-70805-X (pbk.)
    1. Act (Philosophy)   2. Ethics.   3. Communication—Moral and ethical
aspects.   4. Literature—Philosophy.   I. Liapunov, Vadim, 1935–
II. Holquist, Michael, 1935–   .   III. Title.   IV. Series.
BIO5.A35B3413   1993
128'.4—dc20   93-7557

CONTENTS

MICHAEL HOLQUIST

FOREWORD

In his long life under Soviet rule, Bakhtin experienced the whole range of effects an author can produce, from censorship, imprisonment, and banishment to fame and adulation. The shock of his arrest during Stalin's terror made him extremely cautious in later years. It was with the greatest difficulty that a group of young admirers in the early 1960s convinced him to publish again. And it was only after he achieved international acclaim as a result of these publications, and at a time when he knew his death was imminent, that he confessed to his supporters the existence of a cache of his earliest writings. They were hidden away in Saransk, where he lived after returning from his official exile in Kazakhtstan. His young friends were ecstatic in 1972 to learn that Bakhtin had, throughout his many moves, managed to keep with him some of his earliest writings. But when they went to the Mordovian capitol to retrieve the manuscripts, they were horrified to discover them packed away in a lumber room, where rats and seeping water had severely damaged the crude student notepads in which Bakhtin always wrote his books.

After a long period of decipherment and retranscription by yet another devoted band of young disciples, the notebooks were found to contain the fragments of two important projects Bakhtin had undertaken at the outset of his career, when he still thought of himself as working in the tradition of German philosophy. The larger of the two manuscripts was published as *Art and Answerability* by the University of Texas Press in 1990.

The smaller fragment is here published as *Toward a Philosophy of the Act,* translated and annotated by Vadim Liapunov, whose work on the 1990 volume received universal acclaim. The appearance of the present book is an important event for at least two audiences: the increasingly growing number of those who are interested in Bakhtin as the foundational figure in dialogism, a thinker in his own right, and the even larger number of those who are concerned with questions bearing on the relation of philosophy to literary theory, particularly those occupied by the problematic relation of aesthetics and ethics.

For the first group, this text is required reading because it is the earliest of Bakhtin's sustained works, dating from 1919–1921. He was in the midst of all the hardships and exhilaration created by the Revolution's after-effects in Nevel and Vitebsk. There were shortages of food and extraordinary chaos all around, but intellectuals and artists were given a field day. There were several orchestras, staffed by refugees from the former imperial conservatory in St. Petersburg; the art school was enlivened by disputes between Chagall and Malevich. And there were endless public lectures, staged debates, and organized discussions that drew large crowds who wrangled about the eternal questions of God, freedom, justice, and politics. Although Bakhtin even at this time suffered from severe osteomyelitis (and complications arising from a bout of typhus), he was young, vital, and fully engaged in several projects, both private and public.

Toward a Philosophy of the Act is the result of one of those projects. The original manuscript of the present volume was difficult to read not only because of the ravages of time, but because, for the most part, it was written in haste, with some clearer sections in his wife's script, when she took dictation during periods when his bone disease kept Bakhtin from writing in his own hand. In the faded scrawl we can see the race between the occurrence of ideas and their feverish transcription. This volume provides a chance to see Bakhtin in all the heat and urgency of thought as it wrestles with itself. In *Toward a Philosophy of the Act* we catch Bakhtin in the act—the act of creation.

This text further sharpens the profile of Bakhtin's whole career insofar as it demonstrates the depth of his early involvement in the professional discourse of philosophy. More precisely, it reveals new filiations between the themes that first appear here and will guide Bakhtin's thinking throughout the course of his long life. The topics of "authoring," "responsibility," self and other, the moral significance of "outsideness," "participatory thinking," the implications for the individual subject of having "no-alibi in existence," the relation between the world as experienced in actions and the world as represented in discourse—these are all broached here in the white heat of discovery. These themes will be present in more lucid form and specificity in later works, but their suggestiveness and scope will never be greater than they are in the present volume. We are here at the heart of the heart, at the center of the dialogue between being and language, the world and mind, "the given" and "the created" that will be at the core of Bakhtin's distinctive dialogism as it later evolves.

One way to establish the distinctiveness of this work is to contrast it with the project it is seeking to criticize and correct. Much has been made of the youthful Bakhtin's interest in the Marburg school of Neo-Kantianism. What these pages make clear is Bakhtin's obsession not so much with Hermann Cohen and his followers as with Kant himself. We know that during the time he was working on *Toward a Philosophy of the Act,* Bakhtin incessantly read, debated, and lectured on Kant, as he would continue to do after his return in 1924 to Petersburg. Put very crudely, this text is an attempt to detranscendentalize Kant, and more particularly to think beyond Kant's formulation of the ethical imperative.

Kant argued that ethics could be grounded on the principle that all moral agents should make judgments "as if" their consequences did not apply to a particular case involving the agent's own interests, but rather "as if" each judgment might affect any person at any time. Bakhtin calls this principle "the universality of the ought" (p. 100 in original, p. 25 in this translation). Such a principle protects morals from the potential viciousness of unbridled relativity. It therefore has much to recommend it in a post-Enlightenment world no longer able to invoke the authority of an unproblematic God. The principle— a philosophically refined, rationally motivated version of the golden rule, really—continues to be built into most of our current theories of law, as formalized, for instance, in John Rawls' influential ideas in his 1971 *Theory of Justice*.

But Kant's ethic leaves something important out, according to Bakhtin. The system is highly abstract: it gains in authority by marking a distance from the specific, the local—anything, in other words, that has an odor of the subjective about it. Bakhtin in this volume is seeking to get back to the naked immediacy of experience as it is felt from within the utmost particularity of a specific life, the molten lava of events as they happen. He seeks the sheer quality of happening in life before the magma of such experience cools, hardening into igneous theories, or accounts of what has happened. And just as lava differs from the rock it will become, so the two states of lived experience, on the one hand, and systems for *registering* such experience on the other, are fundamentally different from each other. Bakhtin is not talking about the now familiar gap between the order of signs and the order of things so much as meditating the more originary difference between acts (physical and mental) we feel to be uniquely ours in their performance—events occurring in what Bakhtin calls here the "once-occurrent event of Being"—and the consequences of such events. He wants to understand how the constantly aeteiolating difference between what is *now* and what is *after-now* might be bridged in the relation I forge between them in all the singularity of my unique place in existence.

Most of us will intuitively recognize that something is always left out of account when we describe our actions. Bakhtin argues this is not merely a weakness in our own powers of description, but a disunity built into the nature of things. How, then, are the two orders—experience and representation of experience—to be put together? This is a problem other members of Bakhtin's circle in Nevel and Vitebsk were also seeking to solve, and their meetings were devoted to endless discussion of the subject. Bakhtin's philosophical friend Matvei Kagan was using historiography as an example of how an event and its description might be imagined to have coherence; Pumpiansky wrestled with the problem in his readings of Dostoevsky. But it was Bakhtin who attempted to confront the problem head on.

Much of the difficulty of Bakhtin's prose here derives, then, from the complexity of the task he sets himself. He is in a very real sense going back to the point where Kant began his questioning: how can concepts that by definition must be transcendental (in the sense of being independent of any particular experience if they are to organize experience in general) relate to my subjective experience in all its uniqueness? "Possible experience" is a major factor in Kant's system, and one which troubles Bakhtin here greatly. For "possible experience" is an order of experience that is not uniquely mine; it presumes that I can absolutely empathize with another: "Pure empathizing, that is, the act of coinciding with another and losing one's own unique place in once-occurrent Being, presupposes the acknowledgement that my own uniqueness and the uniqueness of my place constitute an inessential moment that has no influence on the character of the essence of the world's being. But this acknowledgement of one's own uniqueness as inessential for the conception of Being has the inevitable consequence that one also loses the uniqueness of Being, and as a result, we end up with a conception of Being only as possible Being, and not essential, actual, once-occurrent, inescapably real Being. This possible Being, however, is incapable of becoming, incapable of living. The meaning of that Being for which my unique place in Being has been acknowledged as inessential will never be able to bestow meaning on me, nor is this the meaning of Being-as-event" (p. 93 of original, pp. 15–16 of translation).

Bakhtin is condemned from the outset by the nature of his subject to perform an impossible task: "All attempts to force one's way from inside the theoretical world and into actual Being-as-event are quite hopeless" (p. 91 of original, p. 12 of translation). Recognizing that all accounts of acts fundamentally differ from those acts as they are actually performed, he nevertheless seeks to describe—the act itself. It is a particularly complex way to demonstrate the truth of the old dictum that states you cannot escape theory, because any opposition to theory is itself ineluctably theoretical. Also, and not coincidentally, Bakhtin here reveals some of the existential pathos that sleeps in such ineluctability.

In his attempt to bridge the chasm between lived act and the "same" act's representation (which is, of course, not at all the same), Bakhtin opposes Kant's principle of "as if," positing instead another principle: that of "no alibi" in existence. The biggest difference between the two (at least at a formal level; there are of course many differences at other levels that are no less defining) can be localized in the ground each presupposes as the basis for ethical action. For Kant, it is the synthesis between sensibility and reason on which his whole system is based. That synthesis requires Kant to postulate the two basic forms of intuition, time and space, and his twelve categories (substance, force, etc.) as necessary transcendentally, insofar as they are prior to any specific act of judgment.

Bakhtin, too, is here seeking a synthesis between sensibility (the lived act, the world of *postupok*) and reason (our discursive systems accounting for, or giving meaning to the act, a world always open to the danger of falling into mere "theoriticism"). But the whole he posits that is capable of containing both is not grounded in a pre-existing structure (the necessary codependence of reason and understanding, personal sensibility and extrapersonal categories that are always prior to specific instances, i.e., Kant's transcendental synthesis).

For Bakhtin, the unity of an act and its account, a deed and its meaning, if you will, is something that is never a priori, but which must always and everywhere be *achieved*. The act is a deed, and not a mere happening (as in "one damned thing after another"), only if the subject of such a *postupok*, from within his own radical uniqueness, weaves a relation *to* it in his accounting *for* it. Responsibility, then, is the ground of moral action, the way in which we overcome the guilt of the gap between our words and deeds, even though we do not have an alibi in existence—in fact, *because* we lack such an alibi: "It is only my non-alibi in being that transforms an empty possibility into an actual answerable act or deed . . ." (p. 113 of original, p. 42 of translation).

One way to think of the importance the non-alibi has for Bakhtin is to think of it not only as a lack that I must fill, but as a lack in Being, a hole in the fabric of the world. The gap Non-alibi seems to name for Bakhtin is something of which we are all aware. It is the space between subjective and objective knowledge which, especially in face of the undoubted power of the exact sciences since the seventeenth century, has manifested itself with increasing frequency. The difference between the order of the mathematical world and the world of human experience has always been recognized. The impersonality of the objective world of geometry was what precisely recommended it to Plato as a model of perfection that could usefully be opposed to the clumsy world of reflections in which actual human beings lived out their brief existences, bewildered by degraded imitations and flickering shadows. The difference between the objective cosmos and our human world was brought home to Roman legionaries every time one of their units was punished with decimation: in the order of numbers, the difference between "nine" and "ten" is purely systemic; for the soldier standing ninth in line it meant life, whereas the "objective" fact of being tenth consigned the next man in line to death. The difference between that event as seen from the perspective of number theory alone and what it meant to an actual legionary on a particular day is the lack Bakhtin's non-alibi seeks to accommodate.

The distinction has become even more profound in post-quantum physics. As Richard Feynman states the case with his usual clarity, "in all the laws of physics that we have found so far there does not seem to be any distinction between the past and future."[1] That is, the laws of gravitation, electricity and magnetism, nuclear interaction, the laws of beta-decay—they are all indifferent to time, insofar as they are in themselves processes that remain the same, even if the order in which they occur is reversed. And yet, if a glass of water falls off a table, none of us expects the drops to reconstitute themselves, the shattered shards to fly together into their previous shape, or the whole complex then to jump off the floor back onto the table.

The most poignant way we manifest our expectation that time is not reversible is in the sure knowledge each of us has that we shall one day die. And yet the glass—and our bodies—are made at the most basic level out of atoms, molecules, and quarks, all of which behave, literally, as if there were no tomorrow—or yesterday. The cold reaches of space, the cosmos as it is understood in theoretical physics, is a space in which human beings are not necessary. It is indeed the case that, as Bakhtin says, "An abyss has formed between the motive of an actually performed act or deed and its product. . . . We have conjured up the ghost of objective culture, and now we do not know how to lay it to rest" (p. 123 in original, pp. 54, 55, 56 in translation).

And yet we cannot, as did some of the so-called Life Philosophers (Dilthey, Bergson), or the Existentialists of the 1950s, ignore the objective world: our world as answerable deed "must not oppose itself to theory and thought, but must incorporate them into itself as necessary moments that are wholly answerable" (p. 123 of original, p. 56 of translation).

This means that "The world in which an act or deed actually proceeds, in which it is actually accomplished, is a unitary and unique world . . . The unitary uniqueness of this world . . . is guaranteed for actuality by the acknowledgment of my unique participation in that world, by my *non-alibi* in it. . . . This world is given to me, from my unique place in Being, as a world that is concrete and unique. For my participative, act-performing consciousness, this world, as an architectonic whole, is arranged around me as around that sole center from which my deed issues or comes forth: I *come upon* this world, inasmuch as I *come forth* or issue from within myself in my performed act or deed of seeing, of thinking, of practical doing" (p. 124 of original, pp. 56–57 of translation).

Bakhtin's *Toward a Philosophy of the Act* is itself an example of what he is here seeking to understand. His deed had a meaning for him as a once-occurrent being in the second decade of this dark century; but the possible slough of subjectivity that act constituted is justified through the resonance it has in a different time and a different place. It is arguably the case that the differences between Italy and Russia, Amalia Riznich and Alexander Pushkin that are analyzed in Bakhtin's reading of Pushkin's 1830 poem are as nothing compared to the differences between the unique site of Vitebsk in 1920 and the United States in 1993, or between the once-occurrent being who was Bakhtin at the moment of this text's composition and the uniqueness of any of us who read the text here and now. But the non-alibi Bakhtin sought to underwrite in this text finds (one of) its justification(s) in the new configuration of the unitary and unique world constituted by the unique appropriation each of us as readers will make of the work. In a time and place dominated by the rediscovery of the potential radicalness of the Kantian tradition, a new turn to "ethical criticism," and the vexed questions raised in cultural criticism by the problem of "situated knowledge," *Philosophy of the Act* will find its own "answerability."

1. Richard Feynman, "The Distinction of Past and Future," in *The World Treasury of Physics, Astronomy, and Mathematics* (Boston: Little, Brown and Company, 1991), p. 148.

VADIM LIAPUNOV

TRANSLATOR'S PREFACE

Toward a Philosophy of the Act is a translation of an unfinished philosophical essay by M. M. Bakhtin (1895–1975) that was published in Russian in 1986 by S. G. Bocharov under the title *K filosofii postupka*.

According to Bocharov, the manuscript has come down to us in very poor condition: the opening pages are missing (hence we do not know the title Bakhtin himself gave to the essay) and a number of words and phrases are barely legible or quite illegible.

We do know what Bakhtin planned to accomplish, for on page 54 in the present volume he provides an outline of the whole essay. It was to comprise four parts, of which he seems to have written only part I (we do not know how complete it is). Part I begins on p. 56 in the present volume; the whole preceding text is, therefore, an introduction (with several pages missing at the beginning).

The opening paragraph of the introduction (in its present truncated form) is a conclusion: "Aesthetic activity as well is powerless . . ." Judging by the immediately following paragraph, we may assume that in the preceding pages Bakhtin dealt not only with aesthetic activity (aesthetic intuition, aesthetic seeing), but also with the activity of discursive theoretical thinking (actualized in the natural sciences and in philosophy) and with the activity of historical description-exposition.

All of these activities have no access to the "event-ness" of Being, no access to Being as ongoing event. (In another context Bakhtin explains that "the ongoing event of Being" is a phenomenological concept, "for being presents itself to a living consciousness as an ongoing event, and a living consciousness actively orients itself and lives in it as in an ongoing event.") All of these activities proceed to establish a radical split between the content/sense of a given act (i.e., its *noema*) and the historical actuality of its being, that is, the actual and once-occurrent performing/experiencing of that act. The given act, however, is an actual *reality* (that is, it participates in the once-occurrent event of Being) only *as an undivided whole*: only this *whole* act is an actual, living participant in the ongoing event of Being.

The ultimate result of splitting off the content of an act from the actual, once-occurrent performing/experiencing of that act is that we find ourselves divided between two non-communicating and mutually impervious worlds: the world of culture (in which the acts of our activity are objectified) and the world of life (in which we actually create, cognize, contemplate, live our lives and die—i.e., the world in which the acts of our activity are actually accomplished once and only once). (The reader should note here Bakhtin's anticipation of Husserl's concept of the *Lebenswelt*.)

Concentrating above all on theoretical cognition and on aesthetic intuition, Bakhtin argues that neither of them has any way of gaining access (from within itself) to Being as ongoing event (i.e., to the world of life), for there is no unity and interpenetration in them between the content or product of an act and the actual historical performance of that act, in consequence of a fundamental and essential abstraction from oneself as participant in establishing any sense and seeing. In aesthetic intuition, just as in theoretical cognition, there exists the same radical non-communication between the object of the act of aesthetic seeing (the object being a *subiectum* and his life) and the *subiectum* who is the bearer/performer of that act of seeing: in the content of aesthetic seeing we will not find the actually performed act of the one who sees.

And yet the integral, whole act of our activity, of our actual experiencing, is two-sided: it is directed to both the content and the being (the actual accomplishment) of the act. The unitary and unique plane where both sides of the act mutually determine each other (i.e., where they form an undivided whole) is constituted by the ongoing, once-occurrent event of Being. To reflect itself in both directions (in its sense and in its being) the act must, therefore, have the unity of two-sided responsibility or answerability: it must answer both for its content/sense and for its being. The answerability for its being constitutes its *moral* answerability, into which the answerability for its content must be integrated *qua* constituent moment. The pernicious disunity and non-interpenetration of culture and life can be overcome only by regaining this integrity of the act of our activity.

For in reality every thought of mine (every lived-experience, every act), along with its content, constitutes an individually answerable deed—*my* individually answerable deed or performance; it is one of my individually answerable deeds out of which my once-occurrent (unique, singular, sole) life is composed as an uninterrupted deed-performance. This individually answerable deed of mine Bakhtin calls *postupok* (etymologically, the noun means "a step taken" or "the taking of a step") in distinction to the more general *akt* (the Russian equivalent of the Latin *actus* and *actum*). Bakhtin's whole (projected) essay is centrally concerned with the phenomenon of my *postupok*, my individually answerable deed or performance, and with the world in which my *postupok* orients itself on the basis of its unique participation in Being as ongoing event (the world of a unique, individual life as a *postupok*).

In translating Bakhtin I needed a great deal of support, encouragement, and advice from friends and colleagues. I am especially grateful to Michael Holquist, Savely Senderovich, James Hart, Nina Perlina, and Caryl Emerson.

S. G. BOCHAROV

INTRODUCTION
TO THE
RUSSIAN EDITION

Among Bakhtin's works published posthumously in the collection
of his essays *Estetika slovesnogo tvorchestva* [The Aesthetics of Verbal
Creation] (Moscow: Iskusstvo, 1979) the text of central importance
is the treatise "Author and Hero in Aesthetic Activity."[1] Bakhtin
worked on this treatise at the beginning of the 1920s but did not
finish it; it has been published from a manuscript which was preserved (unfortunately, in an incomplete form) among his papers.
Bakhtin's papers also included the manuscript of another philosophical treatise which is quite similar in its problematics, basic ideas, and
language to "Author and Hero in Aesthetic Activity." This manuscript was also preserved in an incomplete form, which we are publishing here under the title *K filosofii postupka* [Toward a Philosophy
of the Act].[2]

The text published here represents only the initial part of a more
extensive philosophical project. The text consists of two large frag-

ments. The first fragment is apparently the introduction to a treatise on moral philosophy that was to consist of several parts, according to the plan outlined at the end of the introduction. The first pages of this introduction are missing in the surviving manuscript: the first eight out of fifty-two, according to the author's pagination. The introduction is followed immediately by "part I" (that is how the author entitled it in the manuscript); only the beginning of this part has been preserved (sixteen pages, according to the author's pagination).

Both the content of the text published here and the outlined plan of the whole treatise show that the distinctive philosophical aesthetics presented in "Author and Hero in Aesthetic Activity" was only a part of a larger philosophical project which went well beyond the bounds of aesthetics. This project is concerned with more general questions which lie on the boundary of aesthetics and moral philosophy; it is concerned with what Bakhtin calls the world of human action—"the world of event" [*mir sobytiia*], "the world of the performed act" [*mir postupka*]. The leading category in this projected treatise is "answerability" [*otvetstvennost'*], and the distinctive concretization of it is an image-concept that Bakhtin introduces here—a "non-alibi in Being" [*ne-alibi v bytii*]: a human being has no right to an alibi—to an evasion of that unique answerability which is constituted by his actualization of his own unique, never-repeatable "place" in Being; he has no right to an evasion of that once-occurrent "answerable act or deed" which his whole life must constitute (cf. the ancient parable of the buried talent as a parable of moral transgression).[3]

It is with a discourse on "answerability" that Bakhtin entered the intellectual life of his time in the immediate postrevolutionary years: his earliest known publication (1919) was an article entitled "Art and Answerability."[4] It spoke in a impassioned tone about surmounting the ancient divorce between art and life through their mutual answerability for each other; and this answerability was to be actualized in the individual person, "who must become answerable through and through": "I have to answer with my own life for what I have experienced and understood in art . . ."[5] Bakhtin probably began working on the treatise "Toward a Philosophy of the Act" soon after that programmatic article and it is inspired by the same passion of surmounting "the pernicious non-fusion and non-interpenetration of culture and life" (p. 3 in the present volume). One can feel that passion behind the somewhat difficult technical language of the treatise that reflects, of course, the philosophical trends of the time of its writing. The critical dimension is very pronounced in the text published here: Bakhtin develops a critique of "fatal theoreticism" in the philosophy of that time (in epistemology, in ethics, and in aesthetics) and opposes to it, as a task to be accomplished, the "answerable unity" of thinking and performed action; he also introduces such categories as "action-performing thinking" [*postupaiushchee myshlenie*] and "participative (unindifferent) thinking" [*uchastnoe myshlenie*]. A human being who "thinks participatively" does not "detach [his] performed act from its product" (footnote on p. 19)—that is the main thesis of this distinctive "philosophy of the answerable act or deed" [*filosofiia postupka*], as the author himself defines the content of his treatise in the text published here (p. 28). Based on this definition, we have entitled this text "Toward a Philosophy of the Act" [*K filosofii postupka*], since we do not know the author's own title.

Bakhtin apparently worked on this treatise during his stay in Vitebsk (1920–1924). It is very likely that the Vitebsk periodical *Iskusstvo* [Art] (1 [March 1921]: 23) was referring to this treatise when it reported that "M. M. Bakhtin continues to work on a book devoted to the problems of moral philosophy." In the text published in the present volume we are dealing with the early Bakhtin, at the beginning of his life's career; and we find here the philosophical sources of a number of leading ideas which he continued to develop in the course of more than half a century of his activity as a thinker.

It was in the context of working on his treatise on moral philosophy that Bakhtin began to write the treatise on aesthetics that the reader knows—"Author and Hero in Aesthetic Activity." This treatise was apparently an offshoot from the treatise on moral philosophy and was written somewhat later. The text of "Author and Hero" that has been published in *Estetika slovesnogo tvorchestva* [The Aesthetics of Verbal Creation] did not include an extant fragment of the first chapter, which deals with certain preliminary propositions concerning the human being as the condition of aesthetic seeing in actual life and in art. We are publishing this fragment as well in the present volume (under the title of the whole treatise, "Author and Hero in Aesthetic Activity").[6] The text of "Author and Hero" published in *Estetika slovesnogo tvorchestva* follows immediately after this fragment. The reader will notice the way the content of Bakhtin's "Toward a Philosophy of the Act" spills over into his treatise on aesthetics; there are formulations in both texts that are very similar, and in the two texts we find variants of an analysis of the same poem by Pushkin. It was characteristic for Bakhtin to come back to certain constant leading themes in his philosophical work and to formulate new variants of his favorite ideas. In a draft for a preface to a collection of his works from various years Bakhtin noted: "My love for variations and for a diversity of terms for a single phenomenon."[7] We can also observe this love for variations on certain themes and ideas in the two early texts that are published in the present volume.

The reader should bear in mind that the author himself did not prepare these manuscripts for publication; that is why the exposition in these texts assumes at times the form of thesis-statements and summaries. The manuscripts have come down to us in very poor condition; some words in them could not be deciphered, while others have been deciphered conjecturally (this is indicated by a question mark in brackets after the doubtful word). The difficult labor of deciphering the manuscripts and preparing them for publication was carried out by L. V. Deriugina, S. M. Aleksandrov, and G. S. Bernshtein.

TOWARD A PHILOSOPHY OF THE ACT • • • • •

M. M. BAKHTIN

TOWARD A
PHILOSOPHY
OF THE ACT

[. . .] Aesthetic activity as well is powerless to take possession of that moment of Being which is constituted by the transitiveness and open event-ness of Being.[1] And the product of aesthetic activity is not, with respect to its meaning, actual Being in process of becoming, and, with respect to its being, it enters into communion with Being through a historical act of effective aesthetic intuiting.[2] Aesthetic intuition is unable to apprehend the actual event-ness of the once-occurrent event, for its images or configurations are objectified, that is, with respect to their content, they are placed outside actual once-occurrent becoming—they do not partake in it (they partake in it only as a constituent moment in the alive and living consciousness of a contemplator).[3]

The moment which discursive theoretical thinking (in the natural sciences and in philosophy), historical description-exposition, and aesthetic intuition have in common, and which is of particular importance for our inquiry, is this: all these activities establish a fundamental split between the content or sense of a given act/activity and the historical actuality of its being, the actual and once-occurrent experiencing of it.[4] And it is in consequence of this that the given act loses its valuableness and the unity of its actual becoming and self-determination. This act is truly real (it participates in once-occurrent Being-as-event) only *in its entirety*. Only this *whole* act is alive, exists fully and inescapably—comes to be, is accomplished. It is an actual living participant in the ongoing event of Being: it is in communion with the unique unity of ongoing Being.[5] But this communion or participation does not penetrate its content/sense aspect, which pretends to being able to achieve full and definitive self-determination within the unity of this or that domain of sense or meaning (science, art, history), although, as we showed, these objective domains, apart from the act that brings them into communion with Being, are not realities with respect to their sense or meaning.[6]

And as a result, two worlds confront each other, two worlds that have absolutely no communication with each other and are mutually impervious: the world of culture and the world of life, the only world in which we create, cognize, contemplate, live our lives and die or—the world in which the acts of our activity[7] are objectified and the world in which these acts actually proceed and are actually accomplished once and only once.

An act of our activity, of our actual experiencing, is like a two-faced Janus. It looks in two opposite directions: it looks at the objective unity of a domain of culture and at the never-repeatable uniqueness of actually lived and experienced[8] life. But there is no unitary and unique plane where both faces would mutually determine each other in relation to a single unique unity. It is only the once-occurrent event of Being in the process of actualization that can constitute this unique unity; all that which is theoretical or aesthetic must be determined as a constituent moment in the once-occurrent event of Being, although no longer, of course, in theoretical or aesthetic terms. An act must acquire a single unitary plane to be able to reflect itself in both directions—in its sense or meaning and in its being; it must acquire the unity of two-sided answerability—both for its content (special answerability) and for its Being (moral answerability).[9] And the special answerability, moreover, must be brought into communion with the unitary and unique moral answerability as a constituent moment in it. That is the only way whereby the pernicious non-fusion and non-interpenetration of culture and life could be surmounted.

Every thought of mine, along with its content, is an act or deed that I perform—my own individually answerable act or deed [*postupok*].[10] It is one of all those acts which make up my whole once-occurrent life as an uninterrupted performing of acts [*postuplenie*]. For my entire life as a whole can be considered as a single complex act or deed that I perform: I act, i.e., perform acts, with my whole life, and every particular act and lived-experience is a constituent moment of my life—of the continuous performing of acts [*postuplenie*]. As a performed act, a given thought forms an integral whole: both its content/sense and the fact of its presence in my actual consciousness—the consciousness of a perfectly determinate human being—at a particular time and in particular circumstances, i.e., the whole concrete historicalness of its performance—both of these moments (the content/sense moment and the individual-historical moment) are unitary and indivisible in evaluating that thought as my answerable act or deed.

But one can take its content/sense moment abstractly, i.e., a thought as a universally valid judgment. For this abstract sense-aspect of the thought, the individual-historical aspect (the author, the time, the circumstances, and the moral unity of his life) is completely immaterial, for this universally valid judgment belongs to the theoretical unity of the appropriate theoretical domain, and its place in this unity exhaustively determines its validity. The evaluation of a thought as an individual act or deed takes into account and includes within itself in full the moment constituted by the theoretical validity of a thought *qua* judgment, that is, an evaluation of the validity of the judgment constitutes a necessary moment in the composition of the performed act, although it does not yet exhaust the latter. For the theoretical validity of a judgment, on the other hand, the individual-historical moment—the transformation of a judgment into an answerable act or deed of its author—is completely immaterial. I myself—as the one who is actually thinking and who is answerable for his act of thinking—I am not present in the theoretically valid judgment. The theoretically valid judgment, in all of its constituent moments, is impervious to my individually answerable self-activity. Regardless of the moments we distinguish in a theoretically valid judgment—such as form (the categories of synthesis) and content (the matter, the experiential and sensuous given) or object and content—the validity[11] of all these moments remains completely impervious to the moment constituted by an individual act—a deed performed by the one thinking.

The attempt to conceive *the ought*[12] as the highest formal category (Rickert's affirmation-negation)[13] is based on a misunderstanding. The ought is capable of grounding the actual presence of a *given* judgment in *my* consciousness under given conditions, i.e., the historical concreteness of an individual fact, but *not* the theoretical veridicality-in-itself[14] of the judgment. The moment of theoretical veridicality is necessary, but not sufficient, in order to make a judgment an *ought*-to-be judgment for me; that a judgment is true is not sufficient to make it an *ought*-to-be act [*postupok*] of thinking. Let me make a somewhat crude analogy: the irreproachable technical correctness of a performed act does not yet decide the matter of its moral value. Theoretical veridicality is technical or instrumental in relation to the ought. If the ought were a formal moment of a judgment, there would be no rupture between life and culture as creation, between the act of judgment as a performed deed (a moment in the unity of the context of my once-occurrent life) and the content/sense of a judgment (a moment in some objective theoretical unity of science), and this would mean that there would exist a unitary and unique context of both cognition and life, culture and life (which is not the case, of course). The affirmation of a judgment as a true judgment is an assigning of it to a certain theoretical unity, and this unity is not at all the unique historical unity of my life.

It is pointless to speak of some sort of special *theoretical* ought; insofar as I am thinking, I must think veridically; veridicality or being-true is the ought of thinking. Is it really the case that the moment of the ought-to-be is inherent in veridicality itself? [15] The ought arises only in the correlating of truth (valid in itself) with our actual act of cognition, and this moment of being correlated is historically a unique moment: it is always an individual act or deed [*postupok*] that does not affect in the least the objective theoretical validity of a judgment, an individual act or deed that is evaluated and imputed within the unitary context of a *subiectum*'s once-occurrent actual life. Veridicality alone is not enough for the ought-to-be. But, on the other hand, the *subiectum*'s answering act that issues from within him, the act of acknowledging that the ought is true—this act, too, does not penetrate at all inside the theoretical makeup and validity of a judgment. Why, insofar as I am thinking, *must* I think veridically? The ought-to-be of veridicality does not follow at all from the theoretical-cognitive determination of veridicality. The moment of the ought-to-be is completely absent from the content of that determination and cannot be derived from it; it can only be brought in from outside and fastened on (Husserl).* [16] On the whole, no theoretical determination and proposition can include within itself the moment of the ought-to-be, nor is this moment derivable from it. There is no aesthetic ought, scientific ought, and—beside them—an ethical ought; there is only that which is aesthetically, theoretically, socially valid, and these validities [17] may be joined by the ought, for which all of them are instrumental. These positings gain their validity within an aesthetic, a scientific, or a sociological unity: the ought gains its validity within the unity of my once-occurrent answerable life.

Actually, one cannot speak of any kind of moral, ethical norms, or of any ought with a determinate content (we shall develop this in detail further on). [18] The ought does not have any determinate content; it does not have a specifically theoretical content. The ought may descend upon everything that is valid in its content, but no theoretical proposition contains in its content the moment of the ought, nor is it grounded by the ought. There is no scientific, aesthetic, and other ought, but neither is there a specifically ethical ought in the sense of a totality of norms with a determinate content. Everything that possesses validity, taken from the aspect of its validity, provides the ground for various special disciplines, and there is nothing left for ethics (what one calls "ethical norms" are in the main social positings, and, when appropriate social sciences have been founded, they will be incorporated into those sciences). The ought is a distinctive category of the ongoing performance of acts or deeds [*postuplenie*] or of the actually performed act (and everything is an act or deed that I perform—even thought and feeling); it is a certain attitude of consciousness, the structure of which we intend to disclose phenomenologically.[19] There *are* no moral norms that are determinate and valid in themselves as *moral* norms, but there *is* a moral *subiectum* with a determinate structure (not a psychological or physical structure, of course), and it is upon him that we have to rely: he will know what is marked by the moral ought and when, or to be exact: by the ought as such (for there *is* no specifically moral ought).*[20]

That my answerable self-activity[21] does not penetrate inside the content/sense aspect of a judgment seems to be contradicted by the fact that it is the *form* of a judgment (the transcendent moment in the makeup of a judgment)[22] which constitutes the moment of our reason's self-activity, i.e., that it is *we* who produce the categories of synthesis. We shall be told that we have forgotten Kant's Copernican achievement.[23] Yet is it really the case that transcendent self-activity is the historical and individual self-activity of my performed act [*postupok*], the self-activity for which I am individually answerable? No one, of course, will claim something like that. The discovery of an *a priori* element in our cognition did not open a way out from within cognition, i.e., from within its content/sense aspect, into the historically individual, actual cognitional act; it did not surmount their dissociation and mutual imperviousness, and hence one was compelled to think up a purely theoretical *subiectum* for this transcendent self-activity, a historically non-actual *subiectum*—a universal consciousness, a scientific consciousness, an epistemological *subiectum*.[24] But, of course, this theoretical *subiectum* had to be embodied each time in some real, actual, thinking human being, in order to enter (along with the whole world immanent to him *qua* object of his cognition) into communion with the actual, historical event of Being as just a moment within it.

Thus, insofar as we detach a judgment from the unity constituted by the historically actual act/deed of its actualization[25] and assign it to some theoretical unity, there *is* no way of getting out from within its content/sense aspect and into the ought and the actual once-occurrent event of Being. All attempts to surmount—from within theoretical cognition—the dualism of cognition and life, the dualism of thought and once-occurrent concrete actuality, are utterly hopeless. Having detached the content/sense aspect of cognition from the historical act of its actualization, we can get out from within it and enter the ought only by way of a leap. To look for the actual cogni-⌐ tional act as a performed deed in the content/sense is the same as trying to pull oneself up by one's own hair. The detached content of the cognitional act comes to be governed by its own immanent laws, according to which it then develops as if it had a will of its own. Inasmuch as we have entered that content, i.e., performed an act of abstraction, we are now controlled by its autonomous laws or, to be exact, we are simply no longer present in it as individually and answerably active human beings.

This is like the world of technology: it knows its own immanent law, and it submits to that law in its impetuous and unrestrained development, in spite of the fact that it has long evaded the task of understanding the cultural purpose of that development, and may serve evil rather than good. Thus instruments are perfected according to their own inner law, and, as a result, they develop from what was initially a means of rational defense into a terrifying, deadly, and destructive force. All that which is technological, when divorced from the once-occurrent unity of life and surrendered to the will of the law immanent to its development, is frightening; it may from time to time irrupt into this once-occurrent unity as an irresponsibly destructive and terrifying force.

Insofar as the abstractly theoretical self-regulated world (a world fundamentally and essentially[26] alien to once-occurrent, living historicalness) remains within its own bounds, its autonomy is justified and inviolable. Such special philosophical disciplines as logic, theory of cognition, psychology of cognition, philosophical biology (all of which seek to discover—theoretically, i.e., by way of abstract cognition—the structure of the theoretically cognized world and the principles of that world) are equally justified. But the world as object of theoretical cognition seeks to pass itself off as the whole world, that is, not only as abstractly unitary Being, but also as concretely unique Being in its possible totality. In other words, theoretical cognition tries to construct a first philosophy (*prima philosophia*)*[27] either in the person of epistemology or of theoretical [1 illegible word][28] (of various kinds—biological, physical, etc.). It would be an injustice to think that this represents the predominant tendency in the history of philosophy; it is rather a specific peculiarity of modern times, and one could even say a peculiarity of the nineteenth and twentieth centuries exclusively.

Participative thinking[29] predominates in all great systems of philosophy, either consciously and distinctly (especially in the Middle Ages) or in an unconscious and masked form (in the systems of the nineteenth and twentieth centuries). One can observe a peculiar lightening of the very term "Being" or "Reality." Kant's classical example against the ontological proof, that a hundred real thalers are not equal to a hundred thinkable thalers, has ceased to be convincing.[30] What was historically on hand once and only once in the reality that was determined by me in an once-occurrent manner is, indeed, incomparably heavier. But when it is weighed on theoretical scales (even with the addition of a theoretical constatation of its empirical existence) in detachment from its historically valuative[31] uniqueness, it is highly unlikely that it will prove to be heavier than what is merely thinkable. Historically actual once-occurrent Being is greater and heavier than the unitary Being of theoretical science, but this difference in weight, which is self-evident for a living and experiencing consciousness, cannot be determined in theoretical categories.*[32]

Content/sense abstracted from the act/deed can be formed into a certain open and unitary Being, but this, of course, is not that unique Being in which we live and die, in which our answerable acts or deeds are performed; it is fundamentally and essentially[33] alien to living historicity. I cannot include my actual self and my life (*qua* moment) in the world constituted by the constructions of theoretical consciousness in abstraction from the answerable and individual historical act. And yet such an inclusion is necessary if that world is the *whole* world, *all* of Being (all of Being in principle or as projected,[34] i.e., systematically; the system of theoretical Being may itself remain open, of course). In that world we would find ourselves to be determined, predetermined, bygone, and finished, that is, essentially not living. We would have cast ourselves out of life—as answerable, risk-fraught, and open becoming through performed actions—and into an indifferent and, fundamentally,[35] accomplished and finished theoretical Being (which is not yet completed and is yet to be determined only in the process of cognition, but to be determined precisely as a given). It should be clear that this can be done only if we abstract from that which is absolutely arbitrary (answerably arbitrary) and absolutely new that which is being created and is yet-to-be in a performed act, that is, if we abstract precisely from that whereby a performed act actually lives.

Any kind of *practical* orientation of my life within the theoretical world is impossible: it is impossible to live in it, impossible to perform answerable deeds. In that world I am unnecessary; I am essentially and fundamentally[36] non-existent in it. The theoretical world is obtained through an essential and fundamental abstraction from the fact of my unique being and from the moral sense of that fact—"as if I did not exist." And this concept of Being is indifferent to the central fact—central for me—of my unique and actual communion with Being (I, too, exist), and it cannot in principle add anything to it or subtract anything from it, for it remains equal to itself and identical in its sense and significance, regardless of whether I exist or not; it cannot determine my life as an answerable performing of deeds, it cannot provide any criteria for the life of practice, the life of the deed, for it is *not* the Being *in which I live*, and, if it were the only Being, *I* would not exist.

What follows from this least of all, of course, is any kind of relativism, which denies the autonomy of truth and attempts to turn truth into something relative and conditioned (into some moment alien to it—a constituent moment of practical life, for example) precisely in respect of its being the truth. When considered from our standpoint, the autonomy of truth, its purity and self-determination from the standpoint of method are completely preserved. It is precisely on the condition that it is pure that truth can participate answerably in Being-as-event; life-as-event does not need a truth that is relative from within itself. The validity of truth is sufficient unto itself, absolute, and eternal,[37] and an answerable act or deed of cognition takes into account this peculiarity of it; that is what constitutes its essence. The validity of a theoretical positing does not depend on whether it has been cognized by someone or not. Newton's laws were valid in themselves even before Newton discovered them, and it was not this discovery that made them valid for the first time. But these truths did not exist as *cognized* truths—as moments participating in once-occurrent Being-as-event, and this is of essential importance, for this is what constitutes the sense of the deed that cognizes them. It would be a crude mistake to think that these eternal truths-in-themselves existed earlier, before Newton discovered them, the way America existed before Columbus discovered it. The eternity of truth cannot be contraposed to our temporality as a duration without end, for which our time is but a mere moment or segment.

The temporality of the actual historicity of Being is but a moment of abstractly cognized historicity. The abstract moment of truth's extra-temporal validity can be contraposed to the equally abstract moment constituted by the temporality of the object of historical cognition. But this entire contraposition does not go beyond the bounds of the theoretical world, and it possesses sense and validity only within that world, whereas the extra-temporal validity of the whole theoretical world of truth fits, in its entirety, within the actual historicity of Being-as-event. Fits within it not temporally or spatially, of course (for these are all abstract moments), but as a moment that enriches Being-as-event. Only the Being of cognition in abstract-scientific categories is, in its very principle, alien—theoretically—to the abstractly cognized meaning. The actual act of cognition—not from within its theoretical-abstract product (i.e., from within a universally valid judgment), but as an answerable act or deed—brings any extra-temporal validity into communion with once-occurrent

Being-as-event. However, the common contraposition of eternal truth and our pernicious temporality has a *non-theoretical* meaning, for this proposition includes within itself a slightly valuative flavor and assumes an emotional-volitional character: here is the eternal ˜ truth (and that is good), and here is our transitory and deficient temporal life (and that is bad). But in this case we have to do with an instance of participative thinking (which seeks to overcome its own givenness for the sake of what-is-to-*be*-attained) [38] sustained in a penitent tone; this participative thinking, however, proceeds within that architectonic of Being-as-event which is affirmed and founded *by us*. This is the nature of Plato's conception.* [39]

An even cruder instance of theoreticism is the attempt to include ˜ the world of theoretical cognition within unitary Being in the capacity of psychic being. Psychic being is an abstract product of theoretical thinking, and it is quite inadmissible to conceive the act/deed of actual thinking as a psychic process, and then to incorporate it in theoretical Being along with all its content. Psychic being is an abstract product to the same extent as transcendent validity is. In this case we commit a palpable absurdity, this time purely theoretically: we turn the great theoretical world (the world as the object of all the sciences, of all theoretical cognition) into a moment of the small theoretical world (of psychic being as the object of psychological cognition). Psychology is justified within its own bounds insofar as it knows cognition only as a psychic process and translates into the language of psychic being both the content/sense moment of the cognitional act and the individual answerability of the actual performance of that act. But it commits a crude error both from the purely ˜ theoretical standpoint and from the standpoint of philosophical practice, when it pretends to being *philosophical* cognition and presents its psychological transcription as if it were actual once-occurrent Being, refusing to admit beside itself the equally legitimate transcendent-logical transcription.

What I have least of all to do with in my life-as-deed is psychic being (except for the case where I act [*postupaiu*] as a theorizing psychologist). While acting answerably and productively in mathematics—while working, let us say, on some theorem—I can conceive but by no means accomplish the attempt to operate with a mathematical concept as if it were an instance of psychic being. The work done by a performed act will not be actualized, of course: a performed act lives and moves in a world that is not the psychic world. When I am working on a theorem, I am directed toward its meaning, which I answerably bring into communion with cognized Being (the actual goal of science), and I know nothing and do not have to know anything about a possible psychological transcription of this answerable act that I actually perform, although for the psychologist, from the standpoint of his goals, this transcription is answerably correct.*[40]

A similar instance of theoreticism are the various attempts to bring theoretical cognition into communion with once-occurrent life conceived in biological, economic, and other categories, i.e., all attempts at pragmatism in all its varieties. In all these attempts one theory is turned into a moment of another theory, and not into a moment of actual Being-as-event. A theory needs to be brought into communion *not* with theoretical constructions and conceived life, but with the actually occurring event of moral being—with practical reason, and this is answerably accomplished by everyone who cognizes, insofar as he accepts answerability for every integral act of his cognition, that is, insofar as the act of cognition as *my* deed is included, along with all its content, in the unity of my answerability, in which and by virtue of which I actually live—perform deeds. All attempts to force one's way from inside the theoretical world and into actual Being-as-event are quite hopeless. The theoretically cognized world cannot be unclosed from within cognition itself to the point of becoming open to the actual once-occurrent world. But from the performed act (and not from the theoretical transcription of it) there is a way out into its content/sense, which is received and included from within that actually performed act; for the act is actually performed in Being.

The world as the content of scientific thinking is a distinctive world: it is an autonomous world, yet not a detached world, but rather a world that is incorporated into the unitary and once-occurrent event of Being through the mediation of an answerable consciousness in an actual deed. But that once-occurrent event of Being is no longer something that is thought of, but something that *is*, something that is being actually and inescapably accomplished through me and others (accomplished, *inter alia*, also in my deed of cognizing); it is actually experienced, affirmed in an emotional-volitional manner, and cognition constitutes merely a moment in this experiencing-affirming. Once-occurrent uniqueness or singularity cannot be thought of, it can only be participatively[41] experienced or lived through. All of theoretical reason in its entirety is only a ⟶ moment of practical reason, i.e., the reason of the unique *subiectum*'s moral orientation within the event of once-occurrent Being. This Being cannot be determined in the categories of non-participant theoretical consciousness—it can be determined only in the catego ries of actual communion, i.e., of an actually performed act, in the categories of participative-effective experiencing[42] of the concrete uniqueness or singularity of the world.

A characteristic feature of contemporary philosophy of life [*Lebensphilosophie*],[43] which endeavors to include the theoretical world within the unity of life-in-process-of-becoming, is a certain aestheti-zation of life, and this masks to some degree the obvious incongruity of pure theoreticism (the inclusion of the large theoretical world within a small, also theoretical, world). As a rule, the theoretical and the aesthetic elements are fused in these conceptions of life. This is what characterizes the most significant attempt to construct a philosophy of life—that of Bergson.*[44] The principal shortcoming of all his philosophical constructions (a shortcoming often noted in the literature about him) is the indiscrimination, in his method, of the heterogeneous components of his conception. What also remains unclear in his method is his definition of philosophical intuition, which he opposes to intellectual, analyzing cognition. There can be no doubt that intellectual cognition (theoreticism), nonetheless, enters as a necessary element into the makeup of intuition as it is actually used by Bergson; this was shown exhaustively by Losskii in his excellent book on Bergson.[45] When these intellectual elements are subtracted from intuition, what remains is purely aesthetic contemplation, with a negligible admixture—a homeopathic dose—of ac-

tual participative thinking.[46] Yet the product of aesthetic contemplation is also abstracted from the effective act of contemplation, and is
not essentially necessary[47] for that act. Hence, aesthetic contemplation as well is unable to grasp once-occurrent Being-as-event in its
singularity. The world of aesthetic seeing, obtained in abstraction
from the actual *subiectum* of seeing, is not the actual world in which
I live, although its content-aspect is inserted into a living *subiectum*.
But just as in theoretical cognition, there is the same essential and
fundamental[48] non-communication between the *subiectum* and his
life as the *object* of aesthetic seeing, on the one hand, and the *subiectum* as the *bearer* of the act of aesthetic seeing, on the other.

In the content of aesthetic seeing we shall not find the actually
performed act of the one who sees. What does not penetrate into the
content-aspect of aesthetic seeing is the unitary two-sided reflexion
of the unitary act that illuminates and assigns to a single answerability both the content and the being-as-performance of the act/
deed. From inside this seeing, there is no way out into life. This is
in no way contradicted by the fact that one can turn oneself and one's
own life into a content of aesthetic contemplation. The very act/deed
of such seeing does not penetrate into the content; aesthetic seeing
does not turn into a confession,[49] and if it does, it ceases to be aesthetic seeing. And in fact, there *are* works which lie on the border of
aesthetics and confession (moral orientation within once-occurrent
Being).

An essential moment (though not the only one) in aesthetic contemplation is empathizing[50] into an individual object of seeing—
seeing it from inside in its own essence. This moment of empathizing
is always followed by the moment of objectification, that is, a placing
outside oneself of the individuality understood through empathizing,
a separating of it from oneself, a *return* into oneself. And only this
returned-into-itself consciousness gives form, from its own place, to
the individuality grasped from inside, that is, shapes it aesthetically
as a unitary, whole, and qualitatively distinctive individuality. And
all these aesthetic moments—unity, wholeness, self-sufficiency, distinctiveness—are transgredient[51] to the individuality that is being
determined: from within itself, these moments do not exist for it in

its own life, it does not live by them—for itself. They have meaning and are actualized by the empathizer, who is situated *outside* the bounds of that individuality, by way of shaping and objectifying the blind matter obtained through empathizing. In other words, the aesthetic reflexion of living life is, in its very principle, *not* the self-reflexion of life in motion, of life in its actual aliveness: it presupposes another *subiectum*, a *subiectum* of empathizing, a *subiectum* situated outside the bounds of that life.[52] One should not think, of course, that the moment of pure empathizing is chronologically followed by the moment of objectifying, the moment of forming. Both of these moments are inseparable in reality. Pure empathizing is an abstract moment of the unitary act of aesthetic activity, and it should not be thought of as a temporal period; the moments of empathizing and of objectifying interpenetrate each other.

I empathize *actively* into an individuality and, consequently, I do not lose myself completely, nor my unique place outside it, even for a moment. It is not the object that unexpectedly takes possession of me as the passive one. It is *I* who empathize actively into the object: empathizing is *my* act, and only that constitutes its productiveness and newness (Schopenhauer and music).*[53] Empathizing actualizes something that did not exist either in the object of empathizing or in myself prior to the act of empathizing, and through this actualized something Being-as-event is enriched (that is, it does not remain equal to itself). And this act/deed that brings forth something new can no longer be a reflecting that is aesthetic in its essence, for that would turn it into something located outside the action-performer and his answerability. Pure empathizing, that is, the act of coinciding with another and losing one's own unique place in once-occurrent Being, presupposes the acknowledgment that my own uniqueness and the uniqueness of my place constitute an inessential moment that has no influence on the character of the essence of the world's being. But this acknowledgment of one's own uniqueness as inessential for the conception of Being has the inevitable consequence that one also loses the uniqueness of Being, and, as a result, we end up with a conception of Being only as possible Being, and not essential, actual, once-occurrent, inescapably real Being. This possible Being, however, is incapable of becoming, incapable of living. The meaning of a Being for which my unique place in Being has been acknowledged as inessential will never be able to bestow sense on me, nor is this really the meaning of Being-as-event.

But pure empathizing as such is impossible. If I actually lost myself in the other (instead of two participants there would be one—an impoverishment of Being), i.e., if I ceased to be unique, then this moment of my not-being could never become a moment of my consciousness; non-being cannot become a moment in the being of consciousness—it would simply not exist for me, i.e., being would not be accomplished through me at that moment. Passive empathizing, being-possessed, losing oneself—these have nothing in common with the *answerable* act/deed of self-abstracting or self-renunciation. In self-renunciation I actualize with utmost activeness and in full the uniqueness of my place in Being. The world in which I, from my own unique place, renounce myself does not become a world in which I do not exist, a world which is indifferent, in its meaning, to my existence: self-renunciation is a performance or accomplishment that encompasses Being-as-event. A great symbol of self-activity, the descending[?] of Christ [32 illegible words].[54] The world from which Christ has departed will no longer be the world in which he had never existed; it is, in its very principle, a different world.

This world, the world in which the event of Christ's life and death was accomplished, both in the fact and in the meaning of his life and death—this world is fundamentally and essentially indeterminable either in theoretical categories or in categories of historical cognition or through aesthetic intuition. In the first case we cognize the abstract sense, but lose the once-occurrent fact of the actual historical accomplishment of the event; in the second case we grasp the historical fact, but lose the sense; in the third case we have both the being of the fact and the sense in it as the moment of its individuation, but we lose our own position in relation to it, our ought-to-be participation in it. That is, nowhere do we have the accomplishment in its fullness—in the unity and interpenetration of both the once-occurrent fact-accomplishment-sense-significance *and* our participation in it (for the world of this accomplishment is unitary and unique).

The attempt to find oneself in the product of the act/deed of aesthetic seeing is an attempt to cast oneself into non-Being, an attempt to give up both my self-activity from my own unique place located outside any aesthetic being and the full actualization of it in Being-as-event. The performed act/deed of aesthetic seeing rises above any — aesthetic being—a product of that act—and is part of a different world· it enters into the actual unity of Being-as-event, bringing the aesthetic world as well into communion with Being in the capacity of a constituent moment. Pure empathizing would be, in fact, a falling away of the act/deed into its own product, and that, of course, is impossible.

Aesthetic seeing is a justified seeing, as long as it does not go beyond its own bounds. But insofar as it pretends to being a philosophical seeing of unitary and once-occurrent Being in its event-ness,[55] aesthetic seeing is inevitably doomed to passing off an abstractly isolated part as the actual whole.

Aesthetic empathizing (i.e., not pure empathizing in which one loses oneself, but empathizing that objectifies) cannot provide knowledge of once-occurrent Being in its event-ness; it can provide only an aesthetic seeing of Being that is located outside the *subiectum* (and of the *subiectum* himself as located outside his self-activity, that is, in his passivity). Aesthetic empathizing into the participant of an event is not yet the attainment of a full comprehension of the event. Even if I know a given person thoroughly, and I also know myself, I still have to grasp the truth of our interrelationship, the truth of the uni-tary and unique event which links us and in which we are participants. That is, my place and function and his, *and* our interrelationship in the ongoing event of Being, i.e., I myself and the object of my aesthetic contemplation, must be [1 illegible word] determined within unitary and unique Being [within the unitary unity of Being?] which encompasses both of us equally and in which the act of my aesthetic contemplation is actually performed; but that can no longer be *aesthetic* being.[56] It is only from within that act as *my* answerable deed that there can be a way out into the unity of Being, and *not* from its product, taken in abstraction. It is only from within my participation that the function of each participant can be understood. In the place of another, just as in my own place, I am in the same state of senselessness. To understand an object is to understand my ought in relation to it (the attitude or position I ought to take in relation to it), that is, to understand it in relation to me myself in once-occurrent Being-as-event, and that presupposes my answerable participation, and not an abstracting from myself. It is only from within my participation that Being can be understood as an event, but this moment of once-occurrent participation does not exist inside the content seen in abstraction from the act *qua* answerable deed.

Yet aesthetic being is closer to the actual unity of Being-as-life than the theoretical world is. That is why the temptation of aestheticism is so persuasive. One can live in aesthetic being, and there are those who do so, but they are *other* human beings and not I myself. This is the lovingly contemplated past life of other human beings, and everything situated outside of me is correlated with them. But I shall not find *myself* in that life; I shall find only a double of myself, only someone pretending to be me. All I can do in it is play a role, i.e., assume, like a mask, the flesh of another—of someone deceased. But the aesthetic answerability of the actor and the whole human being for the appropriateness of the role played remains in actual life, for the playing of a role as a whole is an answerable deed performed by *the one playing*, and not the one represented, i.e., the hero. The entire aesthetic world as a whole is but a moment of Being-as-event, brought rightfully into communion with Being-as-event through an answerable consciousness—through an answerable deed by a participant. Aesthetic reason is a moment in *practical* reason.

Thus, neither theoretical cognition nor aesthetic intuition can provide an approach to the once-occurrent real Being of an event, for there is no unity and interpenetration between the content/sense (a product) and the act (an actual historical performance) in consequence of the essential and fundamental[57] abstracting-from-myself *qua participant* in the course of establishing meaning and seeing. It is this that leads philosophical thinking, which seeks to be on principle purely theoretical, to a peculiar state of sterility, in which it, undoubtedly, finds itself at the present time. A certain admixture of aestheticism produces the illusion of greater vitality, but no more than an illusion. To those who wish and know how to think participatively,[†58] it seems that philosophy, which ought to resolve ultimate problems (i.e., which poses problems in the context of unitary and unique Being in its entirety), fails to speak of what it ought to speak. Even though its propositions have a certain validity, they are incapable of determining an answerable act/deed and the world in which it is actually and answerably performed once and only once.

What is at issue here is not just a question of dilettantism, which is unable to appreciate the great importance of what modern philosophy has achieved in developing methodology for particular domains of culture. One can and should acknowledge that in the domain of the special tasks it sets itself modern philosophy (and Neo-Kantianism in particular) has obviously attained great heights and has been able, finally, to work out perfectly scientific methods (something that positivism in all its varieties, including pragmatism, was unable to do). Our time deserves to be given full credit for bringing philosophy closer to the ideal of a scientific philosophy. But this scientific philosophy can only be a specialized philosophy, i.e., a philosophy of the various domains of culture and their unity in the form of a theoretical transcription from within the objects of cultural creation and the immanent law of their development.[*59] And that is why this theoretical philosophy cannot pretend to being a first philosophy,[60] that is, a teaching *not* about unitary cultural creation, but about unitary and once-occurrent Being-as-event. Such a first philosophy does not exist, and even the paths leading to its creation seem to be forgotten. Hence the profound dissatisfaction with modern philosophy on the part of those who think participatively, a dis-

---

[†]That is, those who know how not to detach their performed act from its product, but rather how to relate both of them to the unitary and unique context of life and seek to determine them in that context as an indivisible unity.

satisfaction that compels some of them to have recourse to such a conception as historical materialism which, in spite of all its defects and defaults,[61] is attractive to participative consciousness[62] because of its effort to build its world in such a way as to provide a place in it for the performance of determinate, concretely historical, actual deeds; a striving and action-performing consciousness can actually orient itself in the world of historical materialism. In the present context we shall not deal with the question of the particular [illegitimate substitutions? faults?] and incongruities[63] in method by way of which historical materialism accomplishes its departure from within the most abstract theoretical world and its entry into the living world of the actually performed answerable deed. What is important for us, however, is that it does accomplish this departure, and that is what constitutes its strength, the reason for its success. Still others look for philosophical satisfaction in theosophy, in anthroposophy,[64] and in other similar teachings. These teachings have absorbed a great deal of the real wisdom in the participative thought of the Middle Ages and of the Orient; they are utterly unsatisfactory, however, as unitary conceptions, rather than as simply compilations of particular insights of participative thought through the ages, and they commit the same methodological sin that historical materialism commits: a methodical indiscrimination of what is given and what is set as a task, of what *is* and what *ought* to be.[65]

My participative and demanding consciousness can see that the world of modern philosophy, the theoretical and theoreticized world of culture, is in a certain sense actual, that it possesses validity. But what it can also see is that this world is not the once-occurrent world in which I live and in which I answerably perform my deeds. And these two worlds do not intercommunicate; there is no principle for including and actively involving the valid world of theory and of theoreticized culture in the once-occurrent Being-event of life.[66]

Contemporary man feels sure of himself, feels well-off and clear-headed, where he is himself essentially and fundamentally[67] not present in the autonomous world of a domain of culture and its immanent law of creation. But he feels unsure of himself, feels destitute and deficient in understanding, where he has to do with himself, where he is the center from which answerable acts or deeds issue, in actual and once-occurrent life. That is, we *act* confidently only when we do so not as ourselves, but as those possessed by the immanent necessity of the meaning of some domain of culture.

The course from a premise to a conclusion is traversed flawlessly and irreproachably, for I myself do not exist upon that course. But how and where should one include this process of my thinking, which is internally pure and irreproachable and justified through and through in its entirety? In the psychology of consciousness? Or perhaps in the history of an appropriate science? Or in my material budget—as paid for according to the number of lines that have been realized in it? Or perhaps in the chronological order of my day, as my occupation from five to six? Or in my obligations as a scientist or scholar? But all these contexts and possibilities of sense-bestowing are themselves afloat in a peculiarly airless space, and are not rooted in anything, neither in something unitary nor in something unique.

Contemporary philosophy fails to provide a principle for such an inclusion, and this is what constitutes its state of crisis. The performed act or deed is split into an objective content/sense and a subjective process of performance. Out of the first fragment one creates a single systemic unity of culture that is really splendid in its stringent clarity. Out of the second fragment, if it is not discarded as completely useless (it is purely and entirely subjective once the content/sense has been subtracted), one can at best extract and accept a certain aesthetic and theoretical something, like Bergson's *durée* or *élan vital* [12 illegible words]. But neither in the first world nor in the second is there room for the actual and answerable performance of a deed.

But modern philosophy, after all, does know ethics and practical reason. Even Kant's primacy of practical reason is devoutly observed by contemporary Neo-Kantianism. When we spoke of the theoretical world and opposed it to the answerable act, we said nothing about contemporary ethical constructions, which have to do, after all, precisely with the answerable act. Yet the presence of ethical meaning in contemporary philosophy does not add [1 illegible word] at all; almost the entire critique of theoreticism can be extended to ethical systems as well. That is why we shall not go into a detailed analysis of existing ethical doctrines; we shall speak of certain ethical conceptions (altruism, utilitarianism, Cohen's ethics, etc.)[68] and of the special questions tied up with them in the appropriate contexts of our inquiry. What we still need to do at this point is to show that practical philosophy in its basic trends differs from theoretical philosophy only in the object it deals with, not in its method or mode of thinking, i.e., that it is also thoroughly permeated by theoreticism, whereas for the solution of this problem there is no difference between the various trends.

All ethical systems are usually, and quite correctly, subdivided into content-ethics and formal ethics.[69] We have two fundamental and essential[70] objections against content-ethics, and one against formal ethics. Content-ethics endeavors to find and to ground special moral norms that have a definite content—norms that are sometimes universally valid and sometimes primordially relative, but in any case universal, applicable to everyone. A performed act is ethical only when it is governed throughout by an appropriate moral norm that has a definite universal[71] content.

The first fundamental objection against content-ethics (we have already touched upon it earlier) is this: there *are* no specifically *ethical* norms. Every norm that has a definite content must be specifically grounded in its validity by an appropriate discipline—logic, aesthetics, biology, medicine, one of the social sciences. Of course, if we subtract all the norms grounded specifically by an appropriate discipline, we shall find that ethics contains a certain number of norms (usually passed off as fundamental, moreover) which have not been grounded anywhere (it is even difficult to say sometimes in what discipline they could possibly be grounded), but which, nevertheless, sound quite convincing. In their structure, however, these norms are in no way different from scientific norms, and the addition of the epithet "ethical" does not diminish the necessity of still proving scientifically that they are true. In relation to such norms, this problem of proof remains in force, regardless of whether it will ever be resolved or not: every norm that has a particular content must be raised to the level of a special scientific proposition. Until then, it continues to be no more than a practically useful generalization or conjecture. Future philosophically grounded social sciences (they are at present in a highly deplorable state) will considerably reduce the number of such floating norms not rooted in any scientific unity (ethics itself cannot constitute such a scientific unity, but can only be a compilation of practically useful propositions that are sometimes not proved).

In most cases such ethical norms represent, from the standpoint of method, an indiscriminate conglomeration of various principles and evaluations. Thus the highest proposition of utilitarianism, as regards its scientific validity, is subject to the competence and criticism of three special disciplines: psychology, philosophy of law, and sociology. The ought as such (the transformation of a theoretical proposition into a norm) remains completely unfounded in content-ethics. In fact, content-ethics does not even have a way of approaching it: in asserting the existence of special ethical norms, it merely accepts blindly that the moral ought is inherent in the content of certain propositions as such, that it follows directly from their sense-content, i.e., that a certain theoretical proposition (the highest principle of ethics) can be, in its very sense, an ought-to-be proposition, after having presupposed, of course, the existence of a *subiectum*, of a human being. The ethical ought is tacked on from outside. In other words, content-ethics is incapable of even grasping the problem concealed here. As for the attempts to ground the ought biologically, they are instances of inadequate thinking [72] and are not worth considering.

Hence it should be clear that all norms with a particular content, even those specially[?] proved by science, will be relative in regard to the ought, for it is tacked onto them from outside. As a psychologist, sociologist, or lawyer, I can agree *ex cathedra* with a given proposition, but to assert that it becomes thereby a norm regulating my performed act is to overleap the fundamental problem. That a proposition is valid in itself and that I have the psychological ability to understand is not enough, even for the very fact of my actual *ex cathedra* agreement with the validity of the given proposition—as *my* performed act. What is needed in addition to that is something issuing from within myself, namely, the morally ought-to-be attitude of my consciousness toward the theoretically valid-in-itself proposition. It is precisely this moral attitude of consciousness that content-ethics does not know, as if it overleapt the problem concealed here without seeing it. No theoretical proposition can ground a performed act immediately, not even a thought-act, in its actual performedness. In fact, theoretical thinking does not have to know any norms whatever.

A norm is a special form of the free volition[73] of one person in relation to others, and, as such, it is essentially peculiar only to law (laws) and religion (commandments), where its actual obligatoriness—as a norm—is evaluated not from the standpoint of its sense-content, but from the standpoint of the actual authoritativeness of its source (free volition) or the authenticity and exactness of transmission (references to laws, scriptures, canonical texts, interpretations, verifications of authenticity or—more fundamentally and essentially[74]—the foundations of life, the foundations of legislative power, the proven divine inspiration of scriptures). Its validity with respect to its sense-content is grounded only by the free volition (by the lawmaker or by God). But in the process of its creation (the discussion of its theoretical and practical validity) it is not yet a norm in the consciousness of the one who creates it, but constitutes a theoretical determination (the process of discussion has the following form: will such-and-such be correct or useful, i.e., to the benefit of so-and-so?). In all other domains a norm is simply a verbal form for conveying the adaptation of certain theoretical propositions to a particular end: if you want or need such-and-such, then in view of the fact that . . . (a theoretically valid proposition is invoked here), you must act in such and such a way. What is not involved here is precisely a free volition and, consequently, there is no authority here either: the whole system is open—"*if* you want or need such-and-such." The problem of an authoritative free volition (that creates a norm) is a problem in the philosophy of law, in the philosophy of religion, and constitutes one of the problems of a real moral philosophy as a fundamental science—as a first philosophy (the problem of the lawgiver).*[75]

The second flaw of content-ethics is its universality[76]—the assumption that the ought can be extended, can apply to everyone. This error follows, of course, from the foregoing. Since the content of norms is adopted from a scientifically valid judgment, and the form is illegitimately appropriated from law or from commandments, the universality of norms is completely inevitable. The universality of the ought is a defect which is peculiar to formal ethics as well. Hence we turn now to a consideration of formal ethics.

The radical defect of content-ethics that we examined above is alien to formal ethics (in its principle, of course, as *formal* ethics, and not in its actual, concrete actualization, in which case what usually occurs is that all principles are canceled[?] and norms with a particular content are added on from outside; this is what occurs in Kant as well).[77] Formal ethics starts out from the perfectly correct insight that the ought is a category of consciousness, a form that cannot be derived from some particular "material" content.[78] But formal ethics (which developed exclusively within the bounds of Kantianism) further conceives the category of the ought as a category of theoretical consciousness, i.e., it theoretizes the ought, and, as a result, loses the individual act or deed. And yet the ought is precisely a category of the individual act; even more than that—it is a category of the individuality, of the uniqueness of a performed act, of its once-occurrent compellentness,[79] of its historicity, of the impossibility to replace it with anything else or to provide a substitute for it. The universal validity of the imperative is substituted for its categoricalness,[80] which can be thought of in a manner similar to the way theoretical truth is conceived.

The categorical imperative[81] determines the performed act as a universally valid law, but as a law that is devoid of a particular, positive content: law as such, in itself, or the idea of pure legality, i.e., legality itself is the content of law. The performed act must be conformable to the law. This conception does include moments that are valid: (1) a performed act must be absolutely non-contingent,[82] and (2) the ought is really absolutely compellent or categorical for me. But the concept of legality is incomparably wider and, in addition to the moments indicated, contains moments that are completely incompatible with the ought: juridical universality[83] and the transplantation of its world of theoretical universal validity into the context of the performed act and the ought. These aspects of legality surrender the actually performed act to pure theory, surrender it to the solely theoretical justification of a judgment, and the legality of the categorical imperative as universal and universally valid consists precisely in this theoretical justification of it.[84] And that is exactly what Kant demands: the law, which applies a norm to my act or deed, must be justified as capable of becoming a norm of universal conduct.[85] But the question is—how will this justification be effected? Evidently, only by way of purely theoretical determinations: sociological, economic, aesthetic, scientific. The actual deed is cast out into the theoretical world with an empty demand for legality.

The second shortcoming of formal ethics is this: the will itself prescribes the law to itself. The will itself makes pure conformity to law into its own law—it is a law immanent to the will. We can see here a full analogy with the construction of an autonomous world of culture. The will-as-deed produces the law to which it submits, i.e., it dies as an individual will in its own product. The will describes a circle, shuts itself in, excluding the actual—individual and historical—self-activity of the performed act. We are dealing here with the same illusion as in the case of theoretical philosophy: in the latter we have a self-activity of reason, with which my historical and individually answerable self-activity has nothing in common, and for which this categorical self-activity of reason is passively obligatory, while in the former the same happens with the will. All this distorts, at root, the actual moral ought, and does not provide any approach to the actuality of the act performed.

The will is really active, creatively active, in the performed act, but it does not posit a norm or universal proposition at all. The law is the work of a performed act or deed—a thought-deed. But a thought-deed as well is non-active in that aspect of a proposition which consists of a valid content; it is productively active only at the moment of bringing a valid-in-itself truth into communion with[86] actual historical Being (the constituent moment of being actually cognized—of being acknowledged). A performed act is active in the actual unique product it has produced (in an actual, real deed, in an uttered word, in a thought that has been thought, where, moreover, the abstract validity-in-itself of an actual juridical law is but a constituent moment here). In relation to the law, taken from the aspect of its sense-validity, the self-activity of a performed act is expressed in an actually effected acknowledgment, in an effective affirmation.

Thus, fatal theoreticism (the abstracting from my unique self) occurs in formal ethics as well: its world of practical reason is in reality a theoretical world, and not the world in which an act or deed is actually performed. The deed that has already been performed in the theoretical world (requiring, once again, a solely theoretical consideration) *could* be described and understood (and even that only *post factum*) from the standpoint of the formal ethics of Kant and the Kantians. But formal ethics provides no approach to a living act performed in the real world. The primacy of practical reason is in reality the primacy of one theoretical domain over all the others, and that only because it is a domain of the emptiest and least productive form of what is universal. The law of conformity-to-the-law is an empty formula of pure theoreticism. What a practical reason of this kind is least capable of doing is providing a foundation for a first philosophy. The principle of formal ethics is not the principle of an actually performed act at all, but is rather the principle of the possible generalization of already performed acts in a theoretical transcription of them. Formal ethics itself is not productive and is merely a domain of modern philosophy of culture.[87] It is another matter when ethics seeks to become the logic of social sciences. In that case the transcendental method may become much more productive. But why then call the logic of social sciences "ethics" and speak of the primacy of practical reason? It is not worth arguing over words, of course: a moral philosophy of this kind can be and should be created, but one can and should also create another kind of moral philosophy, which deserves this name even more, if not exclusively.

We have identified as unfounded and as essentially hopeless all attempts to orient first philosophy (the philosophy of unitary and once-occurrent Being-as-event) in relation to the content/sense aspect or the objectified product taken in abstraction from the once-occurrent actual act/deed and its author—the one who is think-ing theoretically, contemplating aesthetically, and acting ethically. It is only from within the actually performed act, which is once-occurrent, integral, and unitary in its answerability, that we can find an approach to unitary and once-occurrent Being in its concrete ac-tuality. A first philosophy can orient itself only with respect to that actually performed act.

The actually performed act—not from the aspect of its content, but in its very performance—somehow knows, somehow possesses the unitary and once-occurrent being of life; it orients itself within that being, and it does so, moreover, in its entirety—both in its content-aspect and in its actual, unique factuality. From within, the performed act sees more than just a unitary context; it also sees a unique, concrete context, an ultimate context, into which it refers both *its own sense* and *its own factuality*, and within which it attempts to actualize answerably the unique truth [*pravda*][88] of both the fact and the sense in their concrete unity. To see that, it is of course necessary to take the performed act *not* as a fact contemplated from outside or thought of theoretically, but to take it from within, in its answerability. This answerability of the actually performed act is the taking-into-account in it of all the factors—a taking-into-account of its sense-validity as well as of its factual performance in all its con-crete historicity and individuality. The answerability of the actually performed act knows a unitary plane, a unitary context in which this taking-into-account is possible—in which its theoretical validity, its historical factuality, and its emotional-volitional tone figure as mo-ments in a single decision or resolution. All these moments, more-over (which are different in their significance when viewed from an abstract standpoint), are not impoverished, but are taken in their fullness and in all their truth [*pravda*]. The performed act has, there-fore, a single plane and a single principle that encompasses all those moments within its answerability.

The answerable act or deed alone surmounts anything hypotheti-cal,[89] for the answerable act is, after all, the actualization of a de-cision—inescapably, irremediably, and irrevocably. The answerably performed act is a final result or summation, an all-round definitive conclusion. The performed act concentrates, correlates, and resolves within a unitary and unique and, this time, *final context* both the sense and the fact, the universal and the individual, the real and the ideal, for everything enters into the composition of its answerable motivation. The performed act constitutes a going out *once and for all* from within possibility as such into *what is once-occurrent*.

What we should fear least of all is that the philosophy of the answerable act or deed will revert to psychologism[90] and subjectivism. Subjectivism and psychologism are direct correlatives of objectivism (logical objectivism) and [1 illegible word] only when the answerable act is abstractly divided into its objective sense and the subjective process of its performance. From within the act itself, taken in its undivided wholeness, there is nothing that is subjective and psychological. In its answerability, the act sets before itself its own truth [*pravda*] as something-to-be-achieved[91]—a truth that unites both the subjective and the psychological moments, just as it unites the moment of what is universal (universally valid) and the moment of what is individual (actual). This unitary and unique truth [*pravda*] of the answerably performed act is posited as something-to-be-attained *qua* synthetical truth [*pravda*].

What is equally unfounded is the fear that this unitary and unique synthetical truth [*pravda*] of the performed act is irrational. The actually performed act in its undivided wholeness is more than rational—it is *answerable*. Rationality is but a moment of answerability, [2–3 illegible words] light that is "like the glimmer of a lamp before the sun" (Nietzsche).

All of modern philosophy sprang from rationalism and is thoroughly permeated by the prejudice of rationalism (even where it consciously tries to free itself from this prejudice) that only the logical is clear and rational, while, on the contrary, it is elemental and blind[92] outside the bounds of an answerable consciousness, just as any being-in-itself is. The clarity and necessary consistency of the logical, when they are severed from the unitary and unique center constituted by answerable consciousness, are blind and elemental forces precisely because of the law inherent in the logical—the law of immanent necessity. The same error of rationalism is reflected in the contraposition of the objective *qua* rational to the subjective, individual, singular *qua* irrational and fortuitous. The entire rationality of the answerable act or deed is attributed here (though in an inevitably impoverished form) to what is objective, which has been abstractly detached from the answerable act, while everything fundamental that remains after that is subtracted, is declared to be a subjective process. Meanwhile, the entire transcendental unity of objective culture is in reality blind and elemental, being totally divorced from the unitary and unique center constituted by an answerable consciousness. Of course, a total divorce is in reality impossible and, insofar as we actually think that unity, it shines with the borrowed light of our answerability. Only an act or deed that is taken from outside as a physiological, biological, or psychological fact may present itself as elemental and blind, like any abstract being. But from within the answerable act, the one who answerably performs the act knows a clear and distinct light, in which he actually orients himself.

The ongoing event[93] can be clear and distinct, in all its constituent moments, to a participant in the act or deed he himself performs. Does this mean that he understands it logically? That is, that what is clear to him are only the universal moments and relations transcribed in the form of concepts? Not at all: he sees clearly *these* individual, unique persons whom he loves, *this* sky and *this* earth and *these* trees [9 illegible words], and the time; and what is also given to him simultaneously is the value, the actually and concretely affirmed value of these persons and these objects. He intuits their inner lives as well as desires; he understands both the actual and the ought-to-be sense of the interrelationship between himself and these persons and objects—the truth [*pravda*] of the given state of affairs—and he understands the ought of his performed act, that is, *not* the abstract law of his act, but the actual, concrete ought conditioned by his unique place in the given context of the ongoing event. And all these moments, which make up the event in its totality, are present to him as something given and as something-to-be-achieved in a unitary light,[94] in a unitary and unique answerable consciousness, and they are actualized in a unitary and unique answerable act. And this event as a whole cannot be transcribed in theoretical terms if it is not to lose the very sense of its being an event, that is, precisely that which the performed act knows answerably and with reference to which it orients itself. It would be a mistake to assume that this concrete truth [*pravda*] of the event that the performer of the act sees and hears and experiences and understands in the single act of an answerable deed is something ineffable, i.e., that it can only be livingly experienced in some way at the moment of performing the act, but cannot be uttered clearly and distinctly. I think that language is much more adapted to giving utterance precisely to that truth, and not to the abstract moment of the logical in its purity. That which is abstract, in its purity, is indeed unutterable: any expression is much too concrete for pure meaning—it distorts and dulls the purity and validity-in-itself of meaning. That is why in abstract thinking we never understand an expression in its full sense.

Historically language grew up in the service of participative thinking and performed acts, and it begins to serve abstract thinking only in the present day of its history. The expression of a performed act from within and the expression of once-occurrent Being-as-event in which that act is performed require the entire fullness of the word: its content/sense aspect (the word as concept) as well as its palpable-expressive[95] aspect (the word as image) and its emotional-volitional aspect (the intonation of the word) in their unity. And in all these moments the unitary full word can be answerably valid, i.e., can be the truth [*pravda*] rather than something subjectively fortuitous. One should not, of course, exaggerate the power of language: unitary and once-occurrent Being-as-event and the performed act that partakes in it are fundamentally and essentially[96] expressible, but in fact it is a very difficult task to accomplish, and while full adequacy is unattainable, it is always present as that which is to *be* achieved.

Hence it should be clear that a first philosophy, which attempts to describe Being-as-event as it is known to the answerable act or deed, attempts to describe *not* the world produced by that act, but the world in which that act becomes answerably aware of itself and is actually performed—that a first philosophy of such a kind cannot proceed by constructing universal concepts, propositions, and laws about this world of the answerably performed act (the theoretical, abstract purity of the act), but can only be a description, a phenomenology of that world.[97] An event can be described only participatively.[98]

⁓   But this world-as-event is not just a world of being, of that which is given:[99] no object, no relation, is given here as something simply given, as something totally on hand, but is always given in conjunction with another given[100] that is connected with those objects and relations, namely, that which is yet-to-be-achieved or determined: "one ought to . . . ," "it is desirable that . . ." An object that is absolutely indifferent, totally finished, cannot be something one becomes actually conscious of, something one experiences actually.

⁓ When I experience an object actually, I thereby carry out something in relation to it: the object enters into relation with that which is to-be-achieved, grows in it—within my relationship to that object. Pure givenness cannot be experienced actually. Insofar as I am actually experiencing an object, even if I do so by thinking of it, it becomes a changing moment in the ongoing event of my experiencing (thinking) it, i.e., it assumes the character of something-yet-to-be-achieved. Or, to be exact, it is given to me within a certain event-unity, in which the moments of what-is-given and what-is-to-be-achieved, of what-is and what-ought-to-be, of being and value, are inseparable. All these abstract categories are here constituent moments of a certain living, concrete, and palpable (intuitable)[101] once-occurrent whole—an event.

Similarly, the living word, the full word, does not know an object as something totally given: the mere fact that I have begun speaking about it means that I have already assumed a certain attitude toward it—not an indifferent attitude, but an interested-effective attitude. And that is why the word does not merely designate an object as a present-on-hand entity, but also expresses by its intonation† my valuative[102] attitude toward the object, toward what is desirable or undesirable in it, and, in doing so, sets it in motion toward that which

---

†An actually pronounced word cannot avoid being intonated, for intonation follows from the very fact of its being pronounced.

is yet-to-be-determined about it, turns it into a constituent moment of the living, ongoing event.

Everything that is actually experienced is experienced as something given and as something-yet-to-be-determined, is intonated, has an emotional-volitional tone, and enters into an effective relationship to me within the unity of the ongoing event encompassing us. An emotional-volitional tone is an inalienable moment of the actually performed act, even of the most abstract thought, insofar as I am actually thinking it, i.e., insofar as it is really actualized in Being, – becomes a participant in the ongoing event.

Everything that I have to do with is given to me in an emotional-volitional tone, for everything is given to me as a constituent moment of the event in which I am participating. Insofar as I have thought of an object, I have entered into a relationship with it that has the character of an ongoing event. In its correlation with me, an object is inseparable from its function in the ongoing event. But this function of the object within the unity of the actual event encompassing us is *its actual, affirmed value*, i.e., is *its emotional-volitional tone*.

Insofar as we abstractly separate the content of a lived-experience from its actual experiencing, the content presents itself to us as something absolutely indifferent to value *qua* actual and affirmed value; even a thought about value can be separated from an actual act of valuation (cf. Rickert's position as regards value).[103] Yet in order to become really actualized and thus made into a participant in the historical being of actual cognition, the valid-in-itself content of a possible lived-experience (a thought) must enter into an essential interconnection with an actual valuation; it is only as an actual value that it is experienced (thought) by me, i.e., can be actually, actively thought (experienced) in an emotional-volitional tone. That content, after all, does not fall into my head like a meteor from another world, continuing to exist there as a self-enclosed and impervious fragment, as something that is not woven into the unitary fabric of my emotional-volitional, my living and effective, thinking-experiencing, in the capacity of an essential moment in that thinking-experiencing. No content would be actualized, no thought would be actually thought, if an essential interconnection were not established between a content and its emotional-volitional tone, i.e., its actually affirmed value for the one thinking. The active experiencing of an experience, the active thinking of a thought, means not being absolutely indifferent to it, means an affirming of it in an emotional-volitional manner. Actual act-performing thinking is *an emotional-volitional thinking, a thinking that intonates, and this intonation permeates in an essential manner all moments of a thought's content.* The emotional-volitional tone *circumfuses the whole content/sense of a thought in the actually performed act and relates it to once-occurrent Being-as-event.* It is precisely the emotional-volitional tone that *orients* within once-occurrent Being— orients and actually affirms the content/sense within once-occurrent Being.

One can, however, try to claim that the interconnection between the validity of content/sense and its emotional-volitional tone is unessential or fortuitous for the one thinking actively. Is it not possible that the impelling emotional-volitional force of my active thinking is simply a lust for glory or elementary greed, while the content of these thoughts consists of abstract epistemological constructions? Does not one and the same thought have completely different emotional-volitional colorations in the different actual consciousnesses of those who are thinking that thought? A thought may be woven into the fabric of my living, actual, emotional-volitional consciousness for completely extraneous reasons that have no necessary connection with the content/sense aspect of the given thought.

There is no doubt that facts of this kind are possible and that they do actually occur. But is it legitimate to conclude from this that the interconnection is in its very principle unessential and fortuitous? To do so would be to acknowledge that the whole history of culture is something fundamentally fortuitous in relation to the world it has created—the world of objectively valid content (cf. Rickert and his assignment of value to goods [*Güter*]).[104] It is unlikely that anyone would maintain the claim—that the world of actually realized meaning is fundamentally fortuitous—all the way to its ultimate conclusion.

Contemporary philosophy of culture[105] is endeavoring to establish this essential interconnection, but it seeks to do so from within the world of culture.[106] Cultural values are values-in-themselves, and the living consciousness should adapt to them, affirm them for itself, because ultimately creation[?] *is* cognition. Insofar as I am creating aesthetically, I acknowledge thereby responsibly the value of that which is aesthetic, and the only thing I must do is acknowledge it explicitly, actually. And when I do this, I reestablish the unity of motive and aim, of actual performing and the sense of its content. This is the way in which a living consciousness becomes a cultural consciousness and a cultural consciousness becomes embodied in a living consciousness. At one time man actually established all cultural values and now is bound by them. Thus the power of the people, according to Hobbes, is exercised at one time only, in the act of renouncing themselves and surrendering themselves to the ruler; after that the people become slaves of their own free decision.[107] Practically, this act of an original decision, the act of establishing values, is located, of course, beyond the bounds of each living consciousness: any living consciousness finds cultural values to be already on hand as given to it, and its whole self-activity amounts to acknowledging their validity for itself. Having acknowledged once the value of scientific truth in all the deeds or achievements of scientific thinking, I am henceforth subjected to its immanent law: the one who says *a* must also say *b* and *c*, and thus all the way to the end of the alphabet. The one who said *one*, must say *two*: he is drawn by the immanent necessity of a series (the law of series). This means that the experiencing of an experience and the emotional-volitional tone can gain their unity only within the unity of culture; outside that unity they are fortuitous. An actual consciousness, to be unitary, must reflect in itself the systematic unity of culture along with an appropriate emotional-volitional coefficient, which can be simply put outside the brackets in relation to every given domain of culture.

Such views are radically unsound for the reasons we already adduced when we discussed the ought. The emotional-volitional tone and an actual valuation do not relate at all to content as such in its isolation, but relate to it in its correlation with me within the once-occurrent event of Being encompassing us. An emotional-volitional affirmation acquires its tone not in the context of culture; all of culture as a whole is integrated in the unitary and once-occurrent context of life in which I participate. Both culture as a whole and every particular thought, every particular product of a living act or deed, are integrated in the once-occurrent, individual context of actual thinking *qua* event. The emotional-volitional tone opens up the self-seclusion and self-sufficiency of the possible content of a thought, makes it a participant in unitary and once-occurrent Being-as-event. Any universally valid value becomes *actually* valid only in an individual context.

— The emotional-volitional tone relates precisely to the *whole* concrete and once-occurrent unity in its entirety. It expresses the entire fullness of a state of being *qua* event at the given moment, and expresses it as that which is *given* as well as *yet-to-be-determined* from within me as an obligatory participant in it. That is why the emotional-volitional tone cannot be isolated, separated out of the unitary and once-occurrent context of a living consciousness as related only to a particular object as such. This is not a universal valuation of an object independently of that unique context in which it is given to me at the given moment, but expresses the whole truth [*pravda*] of the entire situation as a unique moment in what constitutes an ongoing event.

The emotional-volitional tone, encompassing and permeating once-occurrent being-as-event, is not a passive psychic reaction, but is a certain ought-to-be attitude of consciousness, an attitude that is morally valid and answerably active. This is an answerably conscious *movement* of consciousness, which transforms possibility into the actuality of a realized deed (a deed of thinking, of feeling, of desiring, etc.). We use the term "emotional-volitional tone" to designate precisely the moment constituted by my self-activity in a lived-experience—the experiencing of an experience as *mine: I* think— perform a deed by thinking. This term is used in aesthetics but has a more passive signification there. What is important for us is to relate a given lived-experience *to me* as the one who is actively experiencing it. This relating of it to me as the one who is active has a sensuous-valuational and volitional—performative—character and at the same time it is answerably rational. All these moments are given here in a certain unity that is perfectly familiar to anyone who experienced his thought or his feeling as his own answerable deed, i.e., who experienced them *actively*. This term from psychology (which is oriented—in a way that is fatal for it—to a passively experiencing *subiectum*) should not mislead us here. The moment constituted by the performance of thoughts, feelings, words, practical deeds is an actively answerable attitude that I myself assume—an emotional-volitional attitude toward a state of affairs in its entirety, in the context of actual unitary and once-occurrent life.

The fact that this active emotional-volitional tone (permeating everything actually experienced) reflects the whole individual uniqueness of the given moment of an event does not render it in any way impressionistically irresponsible and only speciously valid. It is precisely here that we find the roots of active answerability, *my* answerability: the emotional-volitional tone seeks to express the truth [*pravda*] of the given moment, and that relates it to the ultimate, unitary, and once-occurrent unity.

It is an unfortunate misunderstanding (a legacy of rationalism) to think that truth [*pravda*] can only be the truth [*istina*] that is composed of universal moments; that the truth of a situation is precisely that which is repeatable and constant in it.[108] Moreover, that which is universal and identical (logically identical) is fundamental and essential,[109] whereas individual truth [*pravda*] is artistic and irresponsible, i.e., it isolates the given individuality. Even if one speaks of the active once-occurrent act (the fact), what one really means is its content (self-identical content) and not the moment of the actual and effective performance of the act. But the question is whether this unity will really be a fundamental and essential unity of Being, namely, a self-equivalence or self-identicalness in content and a constant repetition of that identical moment (the principle of series), which is a necessary moment in the concept of unity. But this moment itself is an abstract derivative and, as such, it is determined by a unity that is actual and once-occurrent. In this sense, the very word *unity* should be discarded as being overly theoreticized; not unity, but *uniqueness*, the uniqueness of a whole that does not repeat itself anywhere and the actuality of that whole and hence, for the one who wishes to think that whole, it excludes[?] the category of unity (in the sense of that which is constantly repeated). This would render more intelligible the special category of solely theoretical consciousness, which is completely indispensable and determinate in that whole; but the answerably acting or act-performing consciousness is in communion with or participates in the actual uniqueness as a moment within that uniqueness. The unity of the actual and answerably act-performing consciousness, on the other hand, should not be conceived as the contentual constancy of a principle, of a right, of a law, and even less so of being. The word that would characterize this more accurately is *faithfulness* [being-true-to], the way it is used in reference to love and marriage, except that love should not be understood from the standpoint of the passive consciousness of psychology (if we did, we would be dealing with a feeling that exists constantly in the soul—something like a constantly felt warmth, whereas a constant feeling, constant in respect of its content, does not exist in the actual experiencing of it). The emotional-volitional tone of a once-occurrent actual consciousness is conveyed more aptly by the word *faithfulness* [being-true-to].

One can observe, however, a certain tendency in modern philosophy toward conceiving the unity of consciousness and the unity of being as the unity of a certain value. But in this case as well value is transcribed theoretically, that is, conceived either as the identical content of possible values or as the constant, identical principle of valuation, i.e., a certain stability in content of a possible value or valuation, and thus the fact of the performed act visibly recedes into the background. Yet the whole point at issue is precisely that fact. It is not the content of an obligation that obligates me, but my signature below it—the fact that at one time I acknowledged or undersigned the given acknowledgment. And what compelled me to sign at the moment of undersigning was not the content of the given performed act or deed. This content could not by itself, in isolation, have prompted me to perform the act or deed—to undersign-acknowledge it, but only in correlation with my decision to undertake an obligation—by performing the act of undersigning-acknowledging. And in this performed act the content-aspect was also but a constituent moment, and what decided the matter was the acknowledgment or affirmation—the answerable deed—that had been actually performed at a previous time, etc. What we shall find everywhere is a constant unity of answerability, that is, *not* a constancy in content and *not* a constant law of the performed act (all content is only a constituent moment), but a certain actual fact of acknowledgment, an acknowledgment that is once-occurrent and never-repeatable, emotional-volitional and concretely individual. Of course, all this *can* be transcribed in theoretical terms and expressed as the constant law of the performed act (this can be done owing to the ambiguity of language). But what we would obtain in this way is an empty formula, which itself would require an actual once-occurrent acknowledgment, whereupon it would never return again, in a consciousness, to its identicalness in content. One can, of course, philosophize about that fact of acknowledgment as much as one wants, but only in order to know and remember also the previously effected acknowledgment as having occurred actually and as having been performed by *me myself*, and that presupposes the unity of apperception and my entire apparatus of cognitional unity. But all of this remains unknown to a living and act-performing consciousness: all of this appears only in a theoretical transcription after the fact. For a living act-performing consciousness, all this is no more than the technical apparatus of the actually performed act.

One can even establish a certain inverse proportion between theoretical unity and actual uniqueness or singularity (of Being or of the consciousness of Being). The closer one moves to theoretical unity (constancy in respect of content or recurrent identicalness), the poorer and more universal is the actual uniqueness; the whole matter is reduced to the unity of content, and the ultimate unity proves to be an empty and self-identical possible content. The further individual uniqueness moves away from theoretical unity, the more concrete and full it becomes: the uniqueness of actually occurring Being-as-event, in immediate proximity to which the answerable act or deed is set. Answerable inclusion in the acknowledged once-occurrent uniqueness of Being-as-event is precisely what constitutes the truth

— [*pravda*] of the situation [*polozhenie*]. The moment of what is absolutely new, what has never existed before and can never be repeated, is in the foreground here and constitutes an answerable continuation in the spirit of that whole which was acknowledged at one time.

What underlies the unity of an answerable consciousness is not a principle as a starting point, but the fact of an actual acknowledgment of one's own participation in unitary Being-as-event, and this fact cannot be adequately expressed in theoretical terms, but can only be described and participatively experienced. Here lies the point of origin of the answerable deed and of all the categories of the concrete, once-occurrent, and compellent ought. I, too, *exist* [*et ego sum*]† actually—in the whole and assume the obligation to say *this* word.[110] I, too, participate in Being in a once-occurrent and never-repeatable manner: I occupy a place in once-occurrent Being that is unique and never-repeatable, a place that cannot be taken by anyone else and is impenetrable for anyone else. In the given once-occurrent point where I am now located, no one else has ever been located in the once-occurrent time and once-occurrent space of once-occurrent Being. And it is around this once-occurrent point that all once-occurrent Being is arranged in a once-occurrent and never-repeatable manner. That which can be done by me can never be done by anyone else. The uniqueness or singularity of present-on-hand Being is compellently obligatory.

This fact of *my non-alibi in Being*,[111] which underlies the concrete and once-occurrent ought of the answerably performed act, is not something I come to know of and to cognize[112] but is something I acknowledge and affirm in a unique or once-occurrent manner. The simple cognition of that fact is a reduction of it to the lowest emotional-volitional level of possibility. In cognizing it, I universalize it:[113] *everyone* occupies a unique and never-repeatable place, *any* being is once-occurrent. What we have here is a theoretical positing which tends toward the ultimate limit of becoming completely free

---

†In all the emotional-volitional, performative [*postupochnaia*] fullness of this affirmation.

of any emotional-volitional tone. There is nothing I can do with this theoretical proposition; it does not obligate me in any way. Insofar as I think of my uniqueness or singularity as a moment of my being that is shared in common by *all* Being, I have already stepped outside my once-occurrent uniqueness, I have assumed a position outside its bounds, and think Being theoretically, i.e., I am not in communion with the content of my own thought; uniqueness as a concept can be localized in the world of universal or general concept and, by doing so, one would set up a series of logically necessary correlations.

This acknowledgment of the uniqueness of my participation in Being is the actual and effectual foundation of my life and my performed deed. My active deed affirms *implicite* its own singularity and irreplaceability[114] within the whole of Being, and in this sense it is set, from within itself, into immediate proximity to the borders of that whole and is oriented within it as in a whole. This is not simply an affirmation of myself or simply an affirmation of actual Being, but a non-fused yet undivided affirmation of myself in Being: I participate in Being as its sole actor.[115] Nothing in Being, apart from myself, is an *I* for me. In all of Being I experience only myself—my unique self—as an *I*. All other *I*s (theoretical ones) are not *I* for me, whereas my own unique (non-theoretical) *I participates* in once-occurrent Being: I *exist* [*ego sum*] in it. Furthermore, what is also given here in a non-fused yet undivided form is both the moment of my passivity and the moment of my self-activity:[116] [1] I find myself in Being (passivity) and I actively participate in it; [2] both that which is given to me and that which is yet to be achieved by me: my own uniqueness is given, yet at the same time it exists only to the extent to which it is really actualized by me as uniqueness—it is always in the act, in the performed deed, i.e., is yet to be achieved; [3] both what *is* and what *ought* to be: I *am* actual and irreplaceable, and therefore *must* actualize[117] my uniqueness. It is in relation to the whole actual unity that my unique ought arises from my unique place in Being. I, the one and only I, can at no moment be indifferent (stop participating) in my inescapably, compellently once-occurrent life; I must have my ought. In relation to everything, whatever it might be and in whatever circumstances it might be given to me, I must act from my own unique place, even if I do so only inwardly. My uniqueness, as compellent non-coinciding with anything that is not *I*, always makes possible my own unique and irreplaceable deed in relation to everything that is not *I*. That I, from my unique place in Being, simply see and know another, that I do not forget him, that for me, too, he exists—that is something only I can do for him at the given moment in all of Being: that is the deed which makes his being more complete, the deed which is absolutely gainful and new, and which is possible only for me. This productive, unique deed is precisely what constitutes the moment of the ought in it. The ought becomes possible for the first time where there is an acknowledgment of the fact of a unique person's being from within that person; where this fact becomes a center of answerability—where I assume answerability for my own uniqueness, for my own being.

Of course, this fact may give rise to a rift, it may be impoverished: I can ignore my self-activity and live by my passivity alone. I can try to prove my alibi in Being, I can pretend to be someone I am not. I can abdicate from my *obligative (ought-to-be) uniqueness*.

An answerable act or deed is precisely that act which is performed on the basis of an acknowledgment of my obligative (ought-to-be) uniqueness. It is this affirmation of my non-alibi in Being that constitutes the basis of my life being actually and compellently given *as well as* its being actually and compellently projected as something-yet-to-be-achieved. It is only my non-alibi in Being that transforms an empty possibility into an actual answerable act or deed (through an emotional-volitional referral to myself as the one who is active). This is the living fact of a primordial act or deed which produces for the first time the answerably performed act—produces its actual heaviness, compellentness; it is the foundation of my life as a deed-performing [*postuplenie*], for to *be* in life, to be *actually*, is to *act*, is to be unindifferent toward the once-occurrent whole.[118]

To affirm definitively the fact of my unique and irreplaceable participation in Being is to enter Being precisely where it does not co-incide with itself: to enter the ongoing event of Being.

Everything that has a content/sense—Being as something determinate in its content, value as valid in itself, truth [*istina*], the good, the beautiful, etc.—all these are only possibilities which could be actualized only in an actually performed act on the basis of an acknowledgment of my unique participation. The transition from possibility to once-occurrent actuality is impossible from within content/sense itself. The world of content/sense is infinite and self-sufficient; its being valid in itself makes me myself useless, and my acts or deeds are fortuitous from its standpoint. This is a domain of endless questions, where one of the possible questions is also the question of who is my fellow-being.[119] One cannot begin in this world, for any beginning will be fortuitous—it will sink in this world of sense or meaning. This world has no center, it provides no principle for choice: everything that *is* could also *not* be, could be *different*, if it can be thought simply as something determinate in respect to its content/sense. From the standpoint of sense or meaning, only the endlessness of valuation and absolute restlessness are possible. From the standpoint of the abstract content of a possible value, any object, however good it may be, must be better, and any embodiment represents, from the standpoint of sense, a pernicious and fortuitous limitation. What is necessary is the initiative of an actually performed act in relation to sense, and this initiative cannot be fortuitous. No sense-validity that is valid in itself can be categorical and compellent, as long as I have my alibi in Being. It is only the acknowledgment of my unique participation in Being from my own unique place in Being that provides an actual center from which my act or deed can issue and renders a beginning non-fortuitous; what is required here in an essential way is the initiative of my own act or deed—my own self-activity becomes an essential, an *ought*-to-be self-activity.

But what is also possible is non-incarnated thought, non-incarnated action, non-incarnated fortuitous life as an empty possibility. A life lived on the tacit basis of my alibi in Being falls away into indifferent Being that is not rooted in anything. Any thought that is not correlated with myself as the one who is obligatively unique[120] is merely a passive possibility. It could exist or *not* exist, it could be different: its being in my consciousness has nothing compellent, irreplaceable about it. And what is also fortuitous is the emotional-volitional tone of such an unincarnated thought—unincarnated in my answerability. The only thing that transforms it into my answerable act or deed is the referral of it into the unitary and once-occurrent context of Being-as-event through an actual acknowledgment of my actual participation in the latter. Everything in me—every movement, gesture, lived-experience, thought, feeling—everything must be such an act or deed; it is only on this condition that I actually live, that I do not sever myself from the ontological roots of actual Being. I exist in the world of inescapable actuality, and not in that of contingent possibility.[121]

Answerability is possible not as answerability for sense or meaning in itself, but as answerability for the once-occurrent affirmation (embodiment) or non-affirmation of it. It is possible, after all, to pass around meaning and it is also possible to lead meaning irresponsibly past Being.

The abstract-sense aspect, when it is not correlated with inescapable actual uniqueness, has the character of a project: it is something like a rough draft of a possible actualization or an unsigned document that does not obligate anyone to do anything. Being that is detached from the unique emotional-volitional center of answerability is a rough draft, an unacknowledged possible variant of once-occurrent Being; only through the answerable participation effected by a unique act or deed can one get out of the realm of endless draft versions and rewrite one's life once and for all in the form of a fair copy.

The category of experiencing the actual world, actual Being—as event—is a category of uniqueness or singularity. To experience an object is to have it as something actually unique or singular, but this singularity of the object and of the world presupposes its being correlated with my own uniqueness or singularity. Everything that is universal[122] and pertains to abstract sense also acquires its real heaviness and compellentness only in correlation with actual uniqueness.

Participative (unindifferent) thinking is, in fact, the emotional-volitional understanding of Being in its concrete uniqueness on the basis of a non-alibi in Being. That is, it is an act-performing thinking, a thinking that is referred to itself as to the only one performing answerable deeds.

Here, however, a number of conflicts arise with theoretical thinking and with the world of theoretical thinking. Actual Being-as-event, which is both given and projected[123] as something-to-be-determined in emotional-volitional tones, and which is correlated with the unique center of answerability—actual Being-as-event is determined in its uniquely important, heavy, and compellent event sense (in its truth [*pravda*]) *not* in and by itself, but is determined precisely in *correlation* with my own obligative[124] uniqueness: the compellently actual "face" of the event is determined for me myself from my own unique place. But if this is so, then it follows that there are as many different worlds of the event as there are individual centers of answerability, i.e., unique participative (unindifferent) selves (and their number is vast). If the "face" of the event is determined from the unique place of a participative self,[125] then there are as many different "faces" as there are different unique places. But where, then, is the one unique and unitary "face"? If my relation to the world is essential for the world, that is, my relation or attitude is *actual* in the world owing to its emotional-volitional value, i.e., is *acknowledged* [1 illegible word], then this acknowledged value, the emotional-volitional picture of the world, presents itself to me in one way, whereas to someone else in another way. Or perhaps we have to recognize doubt as constituting a quite distinctive sort of value? Yes, we do recognize doubt as a distinctive value. It is precisely doubt that forms the basis of our life as effective deed-performing, and it does so without coming into contradiction with theoretical cognition. This value of doubt does not contradict in any way the unitary and unique truth [*pravda*]: it is precisely this unitary and unique truth of the world that demands doubt.

It is precisely this truth that requires me to realize in full my unique participation in Being from my own unique place. The unity of the whole conditions the unique and utterly unrepeatable roles of all the participants. Being, as something determinate, finished, and petrified in respect to its content, would destroy countless uniquely valuable personal worlds, yet it is precisely this Being that for the first time produces the unitary event.

An event as unitary and self-equivalent is something that could be read *post factum* by a detached (non-participating) consciousness [126] that is not interested in the event; yet even in this case there still would be something that remains inaccessible to it, namely, the very event-ness of the event. For an actual participant in the occurring event, everything is drawn toward and concentrated around the unique act or deed he is about to perform—in its totally unpredetermined, concrete, unique, and compellent oughtness. The point is that there *is* no contradiction nor does there *have to be* between the valuative world-pictures of every participant, either from within the consciousness of every participant or simply from the unique place occupied by each participant. The truth [*pravda*] of the event is not the truth that is self-identical and self-equivalent in its content [*istina*], but is the rightful and unique position of every participant—the truth [*pravda*] of each participant's actual, concrete *ought*. A simple example should clarify what has been said.

I love another, but cannot love myself; the other loves me, but does not love himself. Each one is right in his own place, and he is right answerably, not subjectively. From my own unique place only I-for-myself constitute an *I*, whereas all others are *others* for me (in the emotional-volitional sense of this word). For, after all, my performed act (and my feeling—as a performed act) orients itself precisely with reference to that which is conditioned by the uniqueness and unrepeatability of my own place. In my emotional-volitional consciousness the other is in his *own* place, insofar as I love him as *another*, and not as myself. The other's love of me sounds emotionally in an entirely different way to me—in my own personal context—than the same love of me sounds to him, and it obligates him and me to entirely different things. Yet there is no contradiction here, of course. A contradiction could arise for some third party, namely, for a non-incarnated, detached (non-participating) consciousness. For that consciousness, there would be self-equivalent values-in-themselves—human beings, and not *I* and the *other*, which sound in a fundamentally and essentially [127] different way from the valuative standpoint.

Nor can a contradiction arise between unique and affirmed value-contexts. What does an "affirmed context of values" mean? It means the totality of values which are valuable not for one or another individual and in one or another historical period, but for all historical mankind. But I, the unique I, must assume a particular emotional-volitional attitude toward all historical mankind: I must affirm it as really valuable for me, and when I do so everything valued by historical mankind will become valuable for me as well. What does it mean to assert that historical mankind recognizes in its history or in its culture certain things as values? It is an assertion of an empty *possibility* of content, no more. Or what concern is it to me that there is an *a* in Being for whom a *b* is valuable? It is an entirely different matter when I participate uniquely in once-occurrent Being in an emotional-volitional, affirmed manner. Insofar as I affirm my own unique place in the unitary Being of historical mankind, insofar as I am its non-alibi, i.e., stand in an active emotional-volitional relationship to it, I assume an emotional-volitional position in relation to the values it recognizes. Of course, when we speak of all historical mankind, we *intonate* these words; we cannot detach ourselves from a particular emotional-volitional relationship to them; they do not coincide for us with their content/sense; they are brought into correlation with a unique participant and begin to glow with the light of actual value.

From my own unique place an approach is open to the whole world in its uniqueness, and for me it is open only from that place. As disembodied spirit, I lose my compellent, ought-to-be relationship to the world, I lose the actuality of the world. Man-in-general does not exist; *I* exist and a particular concrete *other* exists—my intimate,[128] my contemporary (social mankind), the past and future of actual human beings (of actual historical mankind). All these are valuative moments of Being which are valid individually and do not universalize or generalize once-occurrent Being, and they are revealed[?] to me from my unique place in Being as the foundations of my non-alibi in Being. The totality of universal or general knowledge, on the other hand, defines man in general (as *Homo sapiens*). That he is mortal, for example, acquires its value-sense only from my unique place, inasmuch as I die, my fellow-being dies, and all historical mankind dies. And, of course, the emotional-volitional, valuative sense of my death, of the death of an other who is dear to me, and the fact of any actual person's death are all profoundly different in each case, for all these are different moments in once-occurrent Being-as-event. For a disembodied, detached (non-participating) *subiectum*, all deaths may be equal. No one, however, lives in a world in which all human beings are—with respect to value—equally mortal. (One should remember that to live from within myself, from my own unique place in Being, does not yet mean at all that I live only for my own sake. For it is only from my own unique place that *self-sacrifice* is possible, that is, the answerable centrality of myself can be a *self-sacrificing* centrality.)

There *is* no acknowledged self-equivalent and universally valid value, for its acknowledged validity is conditioned *not* by its content, taken in abstraction, but by its being *correlated* with the unique place of a participant. It is from this unique place that all values and any other human being with all his values can be acknowledged, but he must be actually *acknowledged*. A simple theoretical ascertainment of the fact that someone acknowledges some sort of values does not obligate us to do anything and does not take us outside the bounds of Being as something given, outside the bounds of empty possibility, as long as I have not firmly established my own unique participation in that Being.

Theoretical cognition of an object that exists by itself, independently of its actual position in the once-occurrent world from the standpoint of a participant's unique place, is perfectly justified. But it does not constitute ultimate cognition; it constitutes only an auxiliary, technical moment of such ultimate cognition. My abstracting from my own unique place in Being, my *as it were* disembodying of myself, is itself an answerable act or deed that is actualized from my own unique place, and all knowledge with a determinate content (the possible self-equivalent givenness of Being) that is obtained in this way must be incarnated by me, must be translated into the language of participative (unindifferent) thinking, must submit to the question of what obligation the given knowledge imposes upon me—the unique me—from my unique place. That is, it must be brought into correlation with my own uniqueness or singularity on the basis of my non-alibi in Being and in an emotional-volitional tone. Thus knowledge *of* [*znanie*] the content of the object-in-itself becomes a knowledge of it *for me*—becomes a *cognition* [*uznanie*] *that answerably obligates me.*[129] Abstracting from myself is a technical device which finds its justification when I approach it from my actual once-occurrent place in Being, where I, the knower, have become answerable and subject to the ought for my cognition [*uznanie*]. The entire infinite context of possible human theoretical knowledge—science—must become something *answerably known* [*uznanie*] for myself as a unique participant, and this does not in the least diminish and distort the autonomous truth [*istina*] of theoretical knowledge, but, on the contrary, complements it to the point where it becomes compellently valid truth [*pravda*].[130] Such a transformation of knowing-*of* [*znanie*] into answerable cognition [*uznanie*] is far removed from being a matter of its immediate utilization, as a technical or instrumental moment, for satisfying some practical need in lived life. Let me repeat: to live from within oneself does not mean to live for oneself, but means to be an answerable participant from within oneself, to affirm one's compellent, actual non-alibi in Being.

Participation in the being-event of the world in its entirety does not coincide, from our point of view, with irresponsible self-surrender to Being, with being-possessed by Being. What happens in the latter case is that the passive moment in my participation is moved to the fore, while my to-be-accomplished self-activity is reduced. The aspiration of Nietzsche's philosophy reduces to a considerable extent to this possessedness by Being (one-sided participation); its ultimate result is the absurdity of contemporary Dionysianism.* [131]

The actually experienced fact of my actual participation is impoverished here inasmuch as affirmed Being takes possession of the one who affirmed it, that is, empathizing into one's actual participative Being leads to the loss of oneself in it (one cannot be an impostor), to the renunciation of the ought-to-be uniqueness of oneself.

A participative, incarnated consciousness may appear to be limited, narrowly subjective, only when it is opposed to the consciousness of culture as a self-contained consciousness. We are presented as it were with two value-contexts, two kinds of life: the life of the whole boundless world in its entirety that is capable of being cognized only objectively, and my small personal life. The *subiectum* of the first is the world *qua* whole, while the *subiectum* of the second is a fortuitous single *subiectum*. This contraposition, however, is not a mathematical, quantitative contraposition of the boundlessly large world and a very small human being, i.e., of one unit and a vast number of units (beings). One can, of course, carry out this contraposition of the world and a particular human being from the standpoint of universal or general theory, but that is not what constitutes its real sense. Small and large are not purely theoretical categories here; they are purely valuational categories. And the question that should be asked is: on what plane is this valuational juxtaposition actualized in order to be compellent and actually valid? The answer is: only in a participative (unindifferent) consciousness. The impelling inspiration of my small life and the boundless world is that of my participative (unindifferent) non-alibi in Being; this is an answerable expansion of the context of actually acknowledged values from my own unique place. But insofar as I am detached from that unique place, a split arises between the possible boundless world of cognition and the very small world of values that have been acknowledged by me.

It is only from within this small yet compellently actual world that this (in principle infinite) expansion must proceed, but not by way of dissociation and contraposition. For in the latter case, the insignificantly minute world of actuality would be washed on all sides by the waves of empty possibility, and the inevitable result of this empty possibility would be the splitting of my small actuality in two. The unbridled play of empty objectivity is capable of no more than losing the whole present-on-hand, irresolvably compellent actuality; in itself it imparts a merely possible value[?] to the infinite possibilities.[132] This is when the infinitude of cognition is born: instead of bringing all theoretical (possible) knowledge [*poznanie*] of the world[†] into communion with our actual life-from-within as answerable cognition [*uznanie*], we attempt to bring our actual life into communion with a possible, theoretical context, either by identifying as essential only the universal moments in our actual life, or by understanding our actual life in the sense of its being a small scrap of the space and time of the large spatial and temporal whole, or by giving it a symbolic interpretation.

What happens in all these cases is that the living, compellent, and inescapable uniqueness of our actual life is diluted with the water of merely thinkable empty possibility. Loving[?] corporeality[?][133] is declared to be valid only as a moment of infinite matter, toward which we are indifferent, or as an exemplar of *Homo sapiens*, or as a representative of his own ethics, or as an embodiment of the abstract principle of the Eternal Feminine. That which has actual validity always turns out to be a moment of that which is possible: my own life turns out to be the life of man in general, and this latter life turns out to be one of the manifestations of the world's life. All of these infinite value-contexts, however, are not rooted in anything: they are only possible in me independently of objective and universally valid Being. And yet all we need to do is to incarnate answerably this very act of our thinking to its ultimate conclusion—to undersign it—and we shall turn out to be actual participants in Being-as-event from within it, from our own unique place.

Meanwhile, my actually performed act on the basis of my non-alibi in Being (my performed act as thought, as feeling, as practical accomplishment) is actually set into immediate proximity to the ultimate bounds of Being-as-event, and it is oriented in the event of Being as in a unitary and once-occurrent whole. However full of content a thought might be or however concrete and individual a

[†]Even a fact cognized only theoretically is, as a fact, an empty possibility. Yet the whole sense[?] [1 illegible word] of a judgment consists precisely in the fact that it usually does not remain a theoretical judgment, but rather is actually brought into communion with once-occurrent Being. In this context any abstracting from one's actual participation is very difficult.[134]

deed might be, in their small yet actual domain they participate in the boundless whole. And this does not mean at all that I must conceive myself, my deed, and this whole as constituting something determinate in content; that is neither possible nor necessary. My left hand may not know what my right hand is doing, and yet my right hand is accomplishing the truth [*pravda*]. And it does so not in the sense of Goethe's observation: "In everything that we produce properly, we must see a likeness of everything that can be created properly." Here we have one instance of symbolic interpretation on the basis of a parallelism of the two worlds; this parallelism introduces a moment of rituality into a concretely real act or deed.

To orient an act or deed within the whole of once-occurrent Being-as-event does not mean at all that we translate it into the language of highest values, where the concrete, real, participative (unindifferent) event in which the act orients itself immediately is only a representation or reflection of those values. I participate in the event personally, and every object or person with which I have to do in my once-occurrent life participates personally. I *can* perform a political act or a religious ritual in the capacity of a representative, but that already constitutes a specialized action, which presupposes the fact of my having been actually empowered to perform it. But even here I do not definitively abdicate my answerability in person; on the contrary, my representative and empowered status in itself takes into account my personal answerability. The tacit presupposition of life's ritualism is *not* humility, but pride. One has to develop humility to the point of participating in person and being answerable in person. In attempting to understand our whole life as secret representation and every act we perform—as a ritual act, we turn into impostors or pretenders.

Being a representative does not abolish but merely specializes my personal answerability. The actual acknowledgment-affirmation of the whole which I shall represent is my personally answerable act. Insofar as that act is left out and I remain only the bearer of special answerability, I become possessed, and my deed, severed from the ontological roots of personal participation, becomes fortuitous in relation to that ultimate once-occurrent unity in which it is not rooted, just as the domain which specializes my deed is not rooted for me. Such a severing from the once-occurrent context and the loss of once-occurrent participation in the course of specialization are especially frequent in the case of political answerability. The same loss of once-occurrent unity takes place as a result of the attempt to see in every other, in every object of a given act or deed, *not* a concrete uniqueness which participates in Being *personally*, but a representative of a certain large whole. This does not increase the answerability and ontological non-fortuitousness of my performed deed, but, on the contrary, lightens it and in a certain way de-realizes it: the deed is unjustifiably proud, and the only thing this leads to is that the actual concreteness of the compellently actual uniqueness or singularity begins to be decomposed by abstract sense-possibility. In order to root the deed, the personal participation of once-occurrent being and a once-occurrent object must be in the foreground, for even if you are a representative of a large whole, you are a representative first and foremost personally. And that large whole itself is composed not of universal or general moments, but of concretely individual moments.[135]

The compellently and concretely real validity of the performed act in a given once-occurrent context (of whatever kind), that is, the moment of actuality in it, is precisely its orientation within the whole of actual once-occurrent Being.

The world in which a performed act orients itself on the basis of its once-occurrent participation in Being—that is the specific subject of moral philosophy. Yet the act or deed does not know that world as an entity of determinate content; the performed act has to do only with one single person and one single object, where, moreover, this person and this object are given to it in individual emotional-volitional tones. This is a world of proper names, a world of *these* objects and of particular dates of life. A probative description of the world of a once-occurrent life-as-deed, from within the performed deed and on the basis of its non-alibi in Being, would constitute a *confession*, in the sense of an individual and once-occurrent accounting to oneself for one's own actions.

But these concretely individual and never-repeatable worlds of actual act-performing consciousness (of which, *qua* real components, unitary and once-occurrent Being-as-event comes to be composed) include common moments—*not* in the sense of universal concepts or laws, but in the sense of common moments or constituents in their various concrete architectonics. It is this concrete architectonic of the actual world of the performed act that moral philosophy has to describe, that is, *not* the abstract scheme but the concrete plan or design of the world of a unitary and once-occurrent act or deed, the basic concrete moments of its construction and their mutual disposition. These basic moments are I-for-myself, the other-for-me, and I-for-the-other. All the values of actual life and culture are arranged around the basic architectonic points of the actual world of the performed act or deed: scientific values, aesthetic values, political values (including both ethical and social values), and, finally, religious values. All spatial-temporal values and all sense-content values are drawn toward and concentrated around these central emotional-volitional moments: I, the other, and I-for-the-other.

The first part of our inquiry will be devoted to an examination of these fundamental moments in the architectonic of the actual world of the performed act or deed—the world actually experienced, and not the merely thinkable world. The second part will be devoted to aesthetic activity as an actually performed act or deed, both from within its product and from the standpoint of the author as answerable participant,[136] and [2 illegible words] to the ethics of artistic creation. The third part will be devoted to the ethics of politics, and the fourth and final part to religion. The architectonic of that world is reminiscent of the architectonic of Dante's world and of the world of medieval mystery plays (in mystery plays and in tragedy the action is also set into immediate proximity to the ultimate bounds of Being).[137]

The contemporary crisis is, fundamentally, a crisis of contemporary action [*postupok*]. An abyss has formed between the motive of the actually performed act or deed and its product. But in consequence of this, the product of the deed, severed from its ontological roots, has withered as well. Money can become the motive of the deed that constructs a moral system. In relation to the present moment, economic materialism is in the right, although not because the motives of the actually performed act have penetrated inside the product but rather the reverse: the product in its validity walls itself off from the actually performed act in its actual motivation. But the situation cannot be rectified from within the product: it is impossible to break through from here to the actually performed act. It can be rectified only from within that act itself.

The theoretical and aesthetic worlds have been set at liberty, but from within these worlds themselves it is impossible to connect them and bring them into communion with the ultimate unity, i.e., to incarnate them. Since theory has broken away from the actually performed act and develops according to its own immanent law, the performed act itself, having released theory from itself, begins to deteriorate. All the energy of answerable performing is drawn off into the autonomous domain of culture, and, as a result, the performed act, detached from that energy, sinks to the level of elementary biological and economic motivation, that is, loses all its ideal moments: that is precisely what constitutes the state of civilization.[138] The whole wealth of culture is placed in the service of the biological act. Theory consigns the performed act or deed to the realm of brute Being, drains it of all the moments of ideality in it and draws them into its own autonomous self-contained domain, that is, totally impoverishes the actually performed act. This is the source from which Tolstoyism and all forms of cultural nihilism draw their impelling inspiration.[139]

Given this state of affairs, it may seem that what remains, after we subtract the sense-moments of objective culture, is bare biological subjectivity, the act *qua* biological need. That is why it seems that I am objective and spiritual only as a poet or a scientist/scholar [*uchënyi*], i.e., only from within the product I have brought forth. And it is from within these produced objects that my spiritual biography must be constructed; after subtracting that, all that remains is a subjective act. Everything that has objective validity in the performed deed becomes part of that domain of culture to which the object produced by the deed belongs. Extraordinary complexity of the product and elementary simplicity of the motive. We have conjured up the ghost of objective culture, and now we do not know how to lay it to rest.

This is the source of Spengler's critique, the source of his meta-physical memoirs and of his insertion of history into the space be-tween action and its expression in the form of a valid deed.[140] At the basis of an actual deed is a being-in-communion with the once-occurrent unity; what is answerable does not dissolve in what is spe-cialized (politics), otherwise what we have is not an answerable deed but a technical or instrumental action. Such an answerable deed, however, must not oppose itself to theory and thought, but must incorporate them into itself as necessary moments that are wholly answerable. This is not what we find in Spengler. He opposed the deed to theory, and, in order to escape from winding up in a void, he inserts history in the space between them. If we take the contem-porary deed in isolation from self-contained theory, we end up with a biological or with an instrumental act. History will not save it, for it is not rooted in the ultimate once-occurrent unity.

Life can be consciously comprehended[141] only in concrete an-swerability. A philosophy of life can be only a moral philosophy. Life can be consciously comprehended only as an ongoing event, and not as Being *qua* a given. A life that has fallen away from answerability cannot have a philosophy: it is, in its very principle, fortuitous and incapable of being rooted.

I

The world in which an act or deed actually proceeds, in which it is actually accomplished, is a unitary and unique world that is ex-perienced concretely: it is a world that is seen, heard, touched, and thought, a world permeated in its entirety with the emotional-volitional tones of the affirmed validity of values. The unitary uniqueness of this world (its emotional-volitional, heavy, compellent uniqueness, and not its uniqueness with respect to content/sense) is guaranteed for actuality by the acknowledgment of my unique participation in that world, by my *non-alibi* in it. This acknowledged participation of mine produces a concrete ought—the *ought* to realize the whole uniqueness, as the utterly irreplaceable uniqueness of being, in relation to every constituent moment of this being; and that means that my participation transforms every manifestation of myself (feeling, desire, mood, thought) into my own actively answerable deed.

This world is given to me, from my unique place in Being, as a world that is concrete and unique. For my participative,[142] act-performing consciousness, this world, as an architectonic whole, is arranged around me as around that sole center from which my deed issues or comes forth: I *come upon* this world, inasmuch as I *come forth* or issue from within myself in my performed act or deed of seeing, of thinking, of practical doing.

In correlation with my unique place of active issuing-from-within-myself in that world, all thinkable spatial and temporal relations gain a value-center around which they arrange themselves into a certain stable, concrete architectonic whole, and this *possible* unity becomes *actual* uniqueness. My active unique place is not just an abstract geometrical center, but constitutes an answerable, emotional-volitional, concrete center of the concrete manifoldness of the world, in which the spatial and temporal moment—the actual unique place and the actual, once-occurrent, historical day and hour of accomplishment— is a necessary but not exhaustive moment of my actual centrality— my centrality for myself.[143] Planes that are different from the abstract point of view (spatial-temporal determinateness, emotional-volitional tones, meanings) are contracted and concentrated here to form a concrete and unique unity. "High," "above," "below," "finally," "as yet," "already," "it's necessary," "ought to," "farther," "nearer," etc.— all these expressions acquire not just a content/sense, i.e., assume a thinkable—only possible—[character], but acquire an actual, lived-experienced, heavy, and compellent concretely determinate validity or operativeness from the unique place of my participating in Being-as-event. This actual participating from a concretely unique point in Being engenders the real heaviness of time and the intuitable-palpable[144] value of space, makes all boundaries heavy, non-fortuitous, and valid: the world as an actually and answerably experienced unitary and unique whole.

If I abstract myself from the center that constitutes the starting point of my once-occurrent participation in Being, and I do so, moreover, not only from the content-determinateness of my participation (determinateness with respect to time, space, etc.), but also from its being actually, emotionally, and volitionally acknowledged and affirmed, then the concrete uniqueness and compellent actuality of the world will inevitably begin to decompose; it will disintegrate into abstractly universal, merely possible moments and relations, which can be reduced to an equally abstract-universal, merely possible unity. The concrete architectonic of an actually experienced world will be replaced by a non-temporal, non-spatial, non-valuative systematic unity of abstractly universal moments. Every constituent moment of this unity is logically necessary within the system, but the system itself in its entirety is only something relatively possible. It is only in correlation with me myself—the one thinking actively— and as the actually performed act of my answerable thinking that such a system comes to participate in the actual architectonic of the actually experienced world, as one of its constituent moments; it is only then that such a system becomes rooted in the actual and valuatively operative or valid uniqueness of that world. Everything abstractly universal or general is not a moment in the lived-experienced actual world immediately, the way *this* person is, *this* sky, *this* tree; it constitutes such a moment indirectly—as the content/sense aspect of *this* actual, once-occurrent thought, of *this* actual book. It is only in this way that it actually lives and participates, and not in itself, not in its self-sufficiency with respect to sense or meaning.

But is not sense or meaning eternal,[145] whereas *this* actuality of a consciousness and *this* actuality of a book[146] are transitory? Apart from the actualization of meaning, however, the eternity of meaning is but a possible, non-valuative eternity, an eternity without validity. If, after all, this eternity-in-itself of meaning were actually valid with respect to value, then the act of embodying it, of thinking it, the act of its effective actualization by deed-performing thinking, would be superfluous and unnecessary; the eternity of meaning becomes something actually valued—something actually valid or operative—only when it is correlated with that act. Eternal meaning becomes an impelling, actuating value for deed-performing thinking, as a constituent moment of this thinking, only when it is correlated with actuality: the actually valued eternity of *this* thought, *this* book.[147] But here as well the light of value is a borrowed light: what is compellently valuable in the last resort is the actual eternity of concrete actuality itself in its entirety: of *this* human being, *these* human beings and their world with all its actual moments. And it is hence that the eternal meaning of an actually realized thought blazes up with the light of value.

Everything taken independently of, without reference to, the unique center of value from which issues the answerability of a performed act is deconcretized and derealized: it is deprived of its weight with respect to value, it loses its emotional-volitional compellentness, and becomes an empty, abstractly universal possibility.

From the unique place of my participation in Being, unitary time and unitary space are individuated and brought into communion with Being as constituent moments of a concrete, value-governed uniqueness. From the theoretical standpoint, the space and time of my life constitute insignificant segments of unitary time and space (insignificant from the abstractly quantitative standpoint; participative thinking, however, usually introduces a valuative tone here); and, of course, only that guarantees that the sense of their determinations in judgments remains univocal. But from within my participant life these segments acquire a unitary center of value, and that is what transforms actual space and time into a unique, even if open, individuality.[148]

Mathematical time and space guarantee the possible sense-unity of possible judgments (an actual judgment requires actual emotional-volitional interestedness), whereas my actual participation in time and space from my unique place in Being guarantees their inescapably compellent actuality and their valuative uniqueness—invests them, as it were, with flesh and blood. From within my actual participation and in relation to it, all mathematically possible time and space (the possible infinite past and future) becomes valuatively consolidated; it is as if rays of light radiate from my uniqueness and, passing through time, they confirm historical mankind, they permeate with the light of value all possible time and temporality itself as such, for I myself actually partake in temporality. Such determinations of time and space as "infinity," "eternity," "boundlessness," which are so abundant in our emotional-volitional, participative thinking in lived life, do not function at all as purely theoretical concepts in philosophy, in religion, in art, and in actual usage. On the contrary, they are alive in our thinking owing to certain moments of valuative sense that is peculiar to them; they blaze up with the light of value when correlated with my own participant uniqueness.

A reminder is in order here: to live from within myself, to issue from within myself in my deeds, does not mean at all that I live and act for my own sake. The centrality of my unique participation in Being within the architectonic of the actually lived-experienced world does not consist at all in the centrality of a positive[?] value, for which everything else in the world is but an auxiliary factor. I-for-myself constitute the center from which my performed act and my self-activity of affirming and acknowledging any value come forth or issue, for that is the only point where I participate answerably in once-occurrent Being; it is the center of operations, the headquarters of the commander-in-chief directing my possibilities and my ought in the ongoing event of Being. It is only from my own unique place in Being that I *can* be and *must* be active. My confirmed and acknowledged participation in Being is not just passive (the joy of being), but is first and foremost active (the *ought* to actualize my own unique place). This is not a supreme life-value that systematically grounds for me all other life-values as relative values, as values conditioned by that supreme value.

It is not our intention to construct a logically unified system of values with the fundamental value—my participation in Being—situated at the head, or, in other words, to construct an ideal system of various possible values. Nor do we propose to give a theoretical transcription of values that have been actually, historically acknowledged by mankind, in order to establish such logical relations among them as subordination, co-subordination, etc., that is, in order to systematize them. What we intend to provide is not a system and not a systematic inventory of values, where pure concepts (self-identical in content) are interconnected on the basis of logical correlativity. What we intend to provide is a representation, a description of the actual, concrete architectonic of value-governed experiencing of the world—not with an analytical foundation at the head, but with that actual, concrete center (both spatial and temporal) from which valuations, assertions, and deeds come forth or issue, and where the constituent members are real objects, interconnected by concrete event relations[149] in the once-occurrent event of Being (in this context logical relations constitute but one moment along with the concrete spatial, temporal, and emotional-volitional moments).

In order to give a preliminary idea of the possibility of such a concrete, value-governed architectonic, we shall analyze here the world of aesthetic seeing—the world of art. In its concreteness and its permeatedness with an emotional-volitional tone, this world is closer than any of the abstract cultural worlds (taken in isolation) to the unitary and unique world of the performed act. An analysis of this world should help us to come closer to an understanding of the architectonic structure[150] of the actual world-as-event.

The unity of the world in aesthetic seeing is not a unity of meaning or sense—not a systematic unity, but a unity that is concretely architectonic: the world is arranged around a concrete value-center, which is seen and loved and thought. What constitutes this center is the human being: everything in this world acquires significance, meaning, and value only in correlation with man—as that which is human. All possible Being and all possible meaning are arranged around the human being as the center and the sole value; everything (and here aesthetic seeing has no bounds) must be correlated with the human being, must become human. This does not mean, however, that it is the hero of a work who must be presented as a value that has a positive content, in the sense of attaching some positive valuational epithet to him, such as "good," "beautiful," and the like. On the contrary, the epithets may be all negative, the hero may be bad or pitiful or someone defeated and surpassed in every way. Nevertheless, it is upon him that my *interested* attention is riveted in aesthetic seeing, and everything that constitutes the best with respect to content is disposed around *him*—the bad one—as around the one who, in spite of everything, is the sole center of values. In aesthetic seeing you love a human being not because he is good, but, rather, a human being is good because you love him.[151] This is what constitutes the specific character of aesthetic seeing.

The whole topos of values, the whole architectonic of seeing, would be quite different if he was not the one who constituted the center of values. When I contemplate a picture showing the destruction and completely justified disgrace of a person I love, then this picture will be quite different from the one I see when the person destroyed is of no interest to me from the standpoint of value. And this will occur not because I shall be trying to justify him contrary to sense and justice; all that may be excluded, and the picture may be just and realistic in its content. And yet the picture will be different, nevertheless, different in its essential topos, in the valuationally concrete disposition of its parts and details, in its entire architectonic: what I shall see are different value-features, different moments, and a different disposition of these moments, for the concrete center of my act of seeing and forming the picture will be quite different. This will not be a biased, subjective distortion of seeing, for the architectonic of seeing does not affect the content/sense aspect of the event. The event's content/sense aspect, abstractly considered, remains identical and equivalent to itself, while the concrete centers of value may be different (including here the evaluation of meaning from the standpoint of some particular value that has a determinate content—from the standpoint of the good, the beautiful, the true). But this self-identical content/sense aspect is itself only a moment in the entire concrete architectonic as a whole, and the position of this abstract moment is different when the value-centers of seeing are different. After all, when one and the same object (one and the same from the standpoint of its content/sense) is contemplated from different points of a unique space by several different persons, it occupies different places and is differently presented within the architectonic whole constituted by the field of vision of these different persons observing it; its identicalness in meaning, moreover, enters as such into the composition of concrete seeing as one of its moments, except that in this case the identicalness becomes overlaid with individualized and concrete features. But in contemplating the event, the abstract spatial position is only a moment in the unitary position taken by the participant in that event.

Similarly, a value-judgment about one and the same person that is identical in its content ("he is bad") may have different actual intonations, depending on the actual, concrete center of values in the given circumstances: is it him that I actually love or is what is really dear to me that concrete value in relation to which he is a failure, whereas he himself is of no interest to me at all? This difference cannot be expressed abstractly in the form of a particular subordination of values, for this is a concrete architectonic interrelationship. It is illegitimate to substitute a system of logical relations between values (subordination) for a value-governed architectonic, by interpreting the differences in intonation (in the judgment: "he is bad") in the following systematic manner: in the first case the highest value is a person, while the good is a subordinate value, whereas in the second case it is the converse. There can be no such relations between an abstractly ideal concept and an actual, concrete object. It is equally illegitimate to abstract in a human being from his concrete actuality, leaving only a skeleton of meaning (*Homo sapiens*).

Thus, the center of value in the event-architectonic[152] of aesthetic seeing is man as a lovingly affirmed concrete actuality, and not as a something with self-identical content. Moreover, aesthetic seeing does not abstract in any way from the possible standpoints of various values; it does not erase the boundary between good and evil, beauty and ugliness, truth and falsehood. Aesthetic seeing knows all these distinctions and finds them in the world contemplated, but these distinctions are not drawn out of it and placed above it as ultimate criteria, as the principle of viewing and forming what is seen; they remain within that world as constituent moments of its architectonic and are all equally encompassed by an all-accepting loving affirmation of the human being. Aesthetic vision also knows, of course, "principles of selection," but they are all subordinated architectonically to the supreme value-center of contemplation—the human being.

In this sense one could speak of objective aesthetic love[153] as constituting the principle of aesthetic seeing (except that "love" should not be understood in a passive psychological sense). The valued manifoldness of Being as human (as correlated with the human being) can present itself only to a loving contemplation. Only love is capable of holding and making fast all this multiformity and diversity, without losing and dissipating it, without leaving behind a mere skeleton of basic lines and sense-moments. Only un-self-interested love on the principle of "I love him not because he is good, but he is good because I love him," only lovingly interested attention, is capable of generating a sufficiently intent power to encompass and retain the concrete manifoldness of Being, without impoverishing and schematizing it. An indifferent or hostile reaction is always a reaction that impoverishes and decomposes its object: it seeks to pass over the object in all its manifoldness, to ignore it or to overcome it. The very function of indifference biologically consists in freeing us from the manifoldness of Being, diverting us from what is inessential for us practically—a kind of economy or preservation from being dissipated in the manifoldness. And this is the function of forgetting as well.

Lovelessness, indifference, will never be able to generate sufficient power to slow down and *linger intently* over an object, to hold and sculpt every detail and particular in it, however minute. Only love is capable of being aesthetically productive; only in correlation with the loved is fullness of the manifold possible.

With regard to the center of values (with regard to the concrete human being) in the world of aesthetic seeing, one should not distinguish form from content: the concrete human being is both a formal and a contentual principle of seeing—in their unity and interpenetration. This distinction is possible only with regard to categories of abstract content. All abstract formal moments become concrete moments in the architectonic only when they are correlated with the concrete value of the mortal human being.[154] All spatial and temporal relations are correlated with him alone and only in relation to him do they acquire valuative meaning: "high," "far," "above," "below," "abyss," "boundlessness"—all these expressions reflect the life and the intentness of the mortal human being (not in their abstract mathematical signification, of course, but in their emotional-volitional, valuative sense).

Only the value of mortal man provides the standards for measuring the spatial and the temporal orders: space gains body as the possible horizon of mortal man and as his possible environment, and time possesses valuative weight and heaviness as the progression of mortal man's life, where, moreover, the content of the temporal determination as well as its formal heaviness possess the validity of rhythmic progression. If man were not mortal, then the emotional-volitional tone of this progression of life—of this "earlier," "later," "as yet," "when," "never," and the tone of the formal moments of rhythm, would be quite different. If we annihilate the moment constituted by the life of mortal man,[155] the value of what is actually experienced will be extinguished: both the value of rhythm and the value of content. The point here is not, of course, a particular mathematical duration ("threescore years and ten"); *[156] this duration may be as long or as short as one likes. The point is that there are *termini* or limits of life—birth and death, and it is only the fact of the existence of these *termini* that imparts an emotional-volitional coloration to the passing time of a limited life; even eternity possesses a valuative meaning only in correlation with a determinated life.

The best way to clarify the architectonic disposition of the world in aesthetic seeing around a center of values, i.e., the mortal human being, is to give a form-and-content analysis of some particular work. Let us consider Pushkin's lyrical poem "Parting," written in 1830.[157]

Bound for the shores of your distant homeland
You were leaving this foreign land.
In that unforgettable hour, in that sorrowful hour,
I wept before you for a long time.
My hands, growing ever colder,
Strained to hold you back.

My moans implored you not to break off
The terrible anguish of parting.

But you tore away your lips
From our bitter kiss;
From a land of gloomy exile
You called me to another land.
You said: "On the day of our meeting
Beneath an eternally blue sky
In the shade of olive trees,
We shall once more, my beloved, unite our kisses of love."

But there—alas!—where the sky's vault
Shines with blue radiance,
Where the waters slumber beneath the cliffs,
You have fallen asleep forever.
Your beauty and your sufferings
Have vanished in the grave—
And the kiss of our meeting has vanished as well . . .
But I am waiting for that kiss—you owe it to me . . .

There are two active persons in this poem—the lyrical hero (the objectified author) and "she" (Riznich), and, consequently, there are two value-contexts, two concrete reference-points with which the concrete, valuative moments of Being are correlated. The second context, moreover, without losing its self-sufficiency, is valuatively encompassed (affirmed and founded) by the first, and both of these contexts are, in turn, encompassed by the unitary and valuatively affirming aesthetic context of the author-*artist*, who is situated outside the poem's architectonic of seeing the world (*not* the author-*hero*, who is a participant in this architectonic) and outside that of the contemplator. The aesthetic *subiectum*'s (the author's, the contemplator's) unique place in Being, the point from which his aesthetic activity (his objective love of a concrete human being) starts out or issues, has only one determination: his being situated outside [*vne-nakhodimost'*] [158] all of the moments in the architectonic unity [illegible] of aesthetic seeing. And it is this that for the first time creates the possibility for the aesthetic *subiectum* to encompass the entire spatial as well as temporal architectonic through the action of a valuatively unitary affirming and founding self-activity. Aesthetic empathizing (the seeing of a hero or of an object from within them) is actively accomplished from this unique outside-situated place, and it is in this same place that aesthetic reception is accomplished, that is, the affirming and forming of the material that was gained through empathizing—within the bounds of a unitary architectonic of seeing. The *subiectum*'s outside-situatedness (spatial, temporal, and valuative) the fact that the object of empathizing and seeing is *not* I myself—makes possible for the first time the aesthetic activity of forming.

All of the concrete moments in the architectonic are drawn toward and concentrated round the two centers of value (the hero and the heroine) and both are encompassed equally by the affirming, valuative, human aesthetic self-activity in a single event. Let us trace this disposition of the various concrete moments of Being:

> *Bound for the shores of your distant homeland*
> *You were leaving this foreign land . . .*

The shores of the distant homeland are located in the valuative spatial-temporal context of the heroine's life.[159] The homeland is a homeland for *her*, it is in *her* emotional-volitional tone that the possible spatial horizon becomes a homeland (in the concretely valuative sense of the word, in the full sense of the word), and it is in correlation with *her* uniqueness that the space is concretized *qua* event[160] into a "foreign land." And the moment constituted by the movement in space from foreign land to homeland is also presented—accomplished as an event—in *her* emotional-volitional tone. Yet it is concretized here simultaneously in the context of the author's life as an event in the valuative context of *his* life: "you were *leaving*." For her (in her emotional-volitional tone) it would be a returning, that is, what would predominate is a more positive valuative tone. It is from the standpoint of *his* unique place in the ongoing event that she is "leaving." The architectonic moment expressed by the epithet "distant" is also presented in *his* emotional-volitional tone, in the once-occurrent unity of the ongoing event of *his* life. From the standpoint of what is happening, it is not essential that she will have to make a long journey; what *is* essential is that she will be far away from him, although "distantness" has valuative weight in her context as well. What we have here is an interpenetration and unity of events, while the contexts remain valuatively distinct, i.e., they do not fuse together.

This interpenetration and valuative distinctness—the unity of the event—is even more evident in the second half of the first quatrain:

In that unforgettable hour, in that sorrowful hour,
I wept before you for a long time . . .

Both the hour and its epithets ("unforgettable," "sorrowful") have the character of events both for him and for her, they acquire weight in the temporal sequences of his and her determinated, mortal life. But his emotional-volitional tone is predominant. In correlation with him this temporal moment gains body as that hour of his once-occurrent life which is filled by parting.

In the first version of the poem the beginning as well was presented in the valuative context of the hero:

Bound for the shores of a distant foreign land
You were leaving your homeland . . .

Both the foreign land (Italy) and the homeland (Russia) are presented here in the emotional-volitional tone of the author-hero. In correlation with *her* the same space—within the event of her life—occupies the opposite place.

My hands, growing ever colder,
Strained to hold you back . . .

This is presented in the valuative context of the hero. His hands strained to keep her within their spatial environment, in immediate proximity to his body—in immediate proximity to the unique spatial center, i.e., to that concrete center which bestows sense and valuatively consolidates[161] the homeland and the foreign land, the distantness and the nearness, the past, the brevity of the hour and the prolonged weeping, and the eternity of not forgetting.

My moans implored you not to break off
The terrible anguish of parting . . .

Here, too, the author's context is predominant. Both the rhythmic tension and a certain acceleration of the tempo are filled with content here—with the tension of a determined mortal life and the valuative acceleration of that life's tempo in the intense ongoing event.

You said: "On the day of our meeting
Beneath an eternally blue sky . . ."

Her context and his are in a state of intense interpenetration, they are permeated with the unity of the valuative context of mortal humanity: the eternally blue sky exists in the context of every mortal life. Here, however, this moment constituted by an event common to all humanity is not presented directly to the aesthetic *subiectum* (to the author/contemplator situated outside the architectonic of the world within the poem), but is presented from within the contexts of the heroes, that is, it enters as a valuatively affirmed moment into the composition of the event of their future meeting. Their meeting—the *rapprochement* of the concrete valuative centers of life (his and hers) on any plane whatsoever (earthly, heavenly, temporal, non-temporal)—is more important than the event of their closeness within one horizon, within one valuative environment.[162]

The next two quatrains deepen the concretization of their meeting:

But there—alas!—where the sky's vault
Shines with blue radiance,

Where the waters slumber beneath the cliffs,
You have fallen asleep forever.
Your beauty and your sufferings
Have vanished in the grave—
And the kiss of our meeting has vanished as well . . .
But I am waiting for that kiss—you owe it to me . . .

The first three lines of these last two quatrains depict the event-moments [163] of the universally human context of values (the beauty of Italy), which is affirmed within the heroine's context of values (*her* world), and from here it enters, in affirmed form, into the hero's context as well. This is the environment of her once-occurrent death both for her and for him. The possible environment of her life and of the future meeting is transformed here into the *actual* environment of her death. The valuative event-meaning [164] of the world of Italy *for the hero* is that of a world in which she no longer exists, a world illuminated valuatively by her no-longer-being in that world. *For her* it is a world in which she might exist. All of the following lines are presented in the author-hero's emotional-volitional tone, and it is already in the tone of these lines that the last line is anticipated: [165] the certainty that the promised meeting will take place, nevertheless; that the circle is not closed—the circle of the ongoing event of the interpenetration of their valuative contexts. The emotional-volitional tone of the parting and of the unrealized meeting *here* prepares and turns into the tone of the assured and inevitable meeting *there.*

This, then, is the way in which the event-moments [166] of Being are distributed and arranged around the two value-centers. One and the same object (Italy)—one and the same from the standpoint of content/sense—is different as an event-moment in different value-contexts: for her it is a homeland, for him a foreign land; the fact of her departure is for her a returning, while for him it is a leaving, etc. One and the same (self-identical) Italy and the mathematically self-equivalent distance separating it from Russia have entered here into the unity of the ongoing event and are alive within that unity *not* because of their identicalness in content, but because of the unique place they occupy within the unity of the architectonic, where they are arranged around the two unique centers of values.

Would it be legitimate, however, to contrapose the unitary and self-identical Italy as the real and objective Italy to a merely fortuitous Italy, to the subjective experiencing of Italy as a homeland or as a foreign land? The Italy where she sleeps now to the subjectively-individually experienced Italy? A contraposition of this kind is fundamentally wrong. The experiencing of Italy as event[167] includes, as a necessary constituent moment, the actual unity of Italy in unitary and once-occurrent Being. But this unitary Italy gains body (is invested with flesh and blood) only from within my affirmed participation in once-occurrent Being, in which the once-occurrent Italy is a constituent moment. But this event-context[168] of my unique participation is neither closed nor isolated. The value-context, in which Italy is a homeland (*her* context), is a comprehensible and founded context from the standpoint of the author-hero's event-context, in which Italy is a foreign land. Through the hero's participation in Being from his unique place the unitary and self-identical Italy has become consolidated, for him, into a foreign land and—again, for him—into the homeland of his beloved. For she is valuatively affirmed and founded by him, and, consequently, her entire valuative event-context (in which Italy is her homeland) is affirmed and founded by him as well. And all the other possible facets of the event of once-occurrent Italy that is correlated with valuatively affirmed concrete human beings, i.e., the Italy of all mankind, enter into the composition of his participant consciousness from his unique place in Being. To become a moment in an actual consciousness, even a theoretical consciousness (like that of a geographer), Italy must enter into some event-relation[169] with a concretely affirmed value. There is no relativism here whatsoever: the truth [*pravda*] of Being-as-event contains within itself totally the whole extra-temporal absoluteness of theoretical truth [*istina*]. The world's *unity* is a moment in its concrete *uniqueness* and a necessary condition for our thought, taken from the aspect of its content, that is, our thought as a judgment. But for actual thought as a performed act, unity alone is not enough.

Let us consider some other special features in the architectonic of the poem we are analyzing. The heroine's context of values is affirmed and included in the hero's context. The hero is in the actual now of his life's once-occurrent time; the events of parting and of his beloved's death are situated in his once-occurrent past (they are transposed to the plane of remembrance) and, through the present, they are in need of a filled future, they want event-eternity.[170] This consolidates and bestows validity on all temporal limits and relations: participant experiencing of the time of the event. This whole concrete architectonic in its entirety is given to the aesthetic *subiectum* (the artist/contemplator) who is located outside that architectonic. For him the hero and the hero's concrete event-context are correlated with the value of human beings and of the human, insofar as he—the aesthetic *subiectum*—partakes in an affirmed way in once-occurrent Being, where human beings and all that is human constitute a valuative moment. And it is also for him that rhythm comes to life as the valuatively intent flow of the life of mortal man. This entire architectonic, both in its content and in its formal moments, is alive for the aesthetic *subiectum* only insofar as he has really affirmed and founded the value of all that is human.

This, then, is the character of the concrete architectonic of the world in aesthetic seeing. Here the moment of value is conditioned everywhere *not* by logical foundation as a principle, but by the unique place of an object in the concrete architectonic of the event from the standpoint of the unique place of a participant *subiectum*. All these moments are affirmed and founded as constituent moments in the concrete uniqueness of a human being. The spatial, the temporal, the logical, the valuative moments—all are consolidated or "bodied" here in their concrete unity (homeland, distance, the past, was, will be, etc.); all are correlated with a concrete center of values, i.e., are subordinated to it architectonically, and not systematically; all are rendered meaningful and are localized through it and within it. Each and every moment is alive here as a once-occurrent moment, and the unity itself is but a moment in the concrete uniqueness of a human being.

But this aesthetic architectonic that we have described in its fundamental features is the architectonic of the world produced in the aesthetic deed of contemplating, whereas that deed itself and I—the performer of that deed—are both located outside that architectonic, are excluded from it. This is a world of the affirmed existence of *other* beings; I myself—as the one who affirms—do not exist in it. This is a world of unique *others* who *issue* or proceed *from within themselves* and a world of Being that is valuatively correlated with them. These others are *found* by me; I myself, the one and only I, issuing from within myself—I am fundamentally and essentially situated outside the architectonic. I partake in it only as a contemplator, but contemplation is the active, effective situatedness of the contemplator *outside* the object contemplated. The aesthetically contemplated uniqueness of a human being is, in its very principle, *not* my own uniqueness. Aesthetic activity is a participation of a special, *objectified* kind; from within an aesthetic architectonic there *is* no way out into the world of the performer of deeds, for he is located outside the field of objectified aesthetic seeing.

Let us now turn to the actual architectonic of the actually experienced world of life—the world of participant and deed-performing consciousness. What we see first of all is the fundamental and essential architectonic difference in significance between my own once-occurrent uniqueness and the uniqueness of any other—both aesthetic and actual—human being, between the concrete experiencing of myself and my experiencing of another. The concretely affirmed value of a human being and my own value-for-myself are radically different.

We are not speaking here of the abstract value-judgment by disembodied theoretical consciousness, which knows only the universal content/sense value of any individual, any human being. A consciousness of this kind is incapable of engendering a concrete deed that is *not fortuitously* unique; it can engender only a value-judgment about a deed *post factum* as an exemplar of a deed. We are speaking of an effective, concrete valuation by act-performing consciousness, of a valuation as performed act or deed, which seeks its justification not in a system, but in unique and concrete, never-to-be-repeated actuality. This consciousness contraposes itself, for itself, to all others—

as *others* for itself; contraposes its own I as issuing from within itself to all other unique human beings that it comes upon or finds; contraposes me myself as participant to the world in which I participate, and in that world to all other human beings. I, as once-occurrent, issue or come forth from within myself, whereas all others I find on hand, I come upon them: this constitutes a profound ontological difference in significance within the event of Being.

The highest architectonic principle of the actual world of the performed act or deed is the concrete and architectonically valid or operative contraposition of *I* and the *other*. Life knows two value-centers that are fundamentally and essentially different, yet are correlated with each other: myself and the other; and it is around these centers that all of the concrete moments of Being are distributed and arranged. One and the same object (identical in its content) is a moment of Being that presents itself differently from the valuative standpoint when correlated with me or when correlated with another. And the whole world that is unitary in content, when correlated with me or with another, is permeated with a completely different emotional-volitional tone, is valuatively operative or valid in a different way in the most vital, essential sense. This does not disrupt the world's unity of meaning, but, rather, raises it to the level of a unique event.

This two-plane character of the valuative determinateness of the world—for myself and for the other—is much deeper and much more essential than the difference in the determination of an object which we observed within the world of aesthetic seeing, where one and the same Italy proved to be a homeland for one person and a foreign land for another. Within that world these differences in validity are architectonic, but all of them lie in one dimension—in the world of those who are *others* for me. It is an architectonic interrelationship of two valuatively affirmed *others*. Both Italy-as-homeland and Italy-as-foreign-land are maintained in one tonality, both are located in the world which is correlated with the *other*. The world that is correlated with me is fundamentally and essentially incapable of becoming part of an aesthetic architectonic. As we shall see in detail later on, to contemplate aesthetically means to refer an object to the valuative plane of the *other*.[171]

This valuative architectonic division of the world into *I* and those who are all *others* for me is not passive and fortuitous, but is an active and ought-to-be division. This architectonic is something-*given* as well as something-*to-be-accomplished*,[172] for it is the architectonic of an event. It is not given as a finished and rigidified architectonic, into which I am placed passively. It is the yet-to-be-realized plane of my orientation in Being-as-event or an architectonic that is incessantly and actively realized through my answerable deed, upbuilt by my deed and possessing stability only in the answerability of my deed. The concrete ought is an architectonic ought: the ought to actualize one's unique place in once-occurrent Being-as-event. And it is determined first and foremost as a contraposition of *I* and the *other*.

This architectonic contraposition is accomplished by every moral act or deed, and it is understood by elementary moral consciousness. Yet theoretical ethics has no adequate form for its expression. The form of a general proposition, norm, or law is fundamentally and essentially incapable of expressing this contraposition, the sense of which is absolute self-exclusion.[173] What inevitably arises in this case is an equivocation, a contradiction between form and content. This moment can be expressed only in the form of a description of the concrete architectonic relationship, but such a description is still unknown in moral philosophy. Whence it does not follow at all, of course, that the contraposition of *I* and the *other* has never been expressed and stated—this is, after all, the sense of all Christian morality, and it is the starting point for altruistic morality.[174] But this [3 illegible words] principle of morality has still not found an adequate scientific expression, nor has it been thought through essentially and fully.

• • • • • • • • •

NOTES

INTRODUCTION TO THE RUSSIAN EDITION

1. The works that make up the 1979 collection, to which Bocharov is referring, have been translated into English and published in two separate collections: M. M. Bakhtin, *Speech Genres and Other Late Essays*, tr. Vern W. McGee (Austin: University of Texas Press, 1986), and *Art and Answerability: Early Philosophical Essays* by M. M. Bakhtin, tr. Vadim Liapunov (Austin: University of Texas Press, 1990). "Author and Hero in Aesthetic Activity" appears in the latter collection (pp. 4–231).

2. The Russian original of "Toward a Philosophy of the Act" was published in the yearbook of the Scientific Council of Philosophical and Social Problems of Science and Technology (Academy of Sciences of the USSR) in 1986: *Filosofiia i sotsiologiia nauki i tekhniki: Ezhegodnik 1984–85* (Moscow: Nauka, 1986, pp. 82–138). In addition, this yearbook includes a fragment of the first chapter of "Author and Hero in Aesthetic Activity" (pp. 138–157) that was not published in the 1979 collection *Estetika slovesnogo tvorchestva*

• •

77

[The Aesthetics of Verbal Creation]. The notes to the two texts published in the yearbook are by S. Averintsev (pp. 157–160). Bocharov's introduction is on pp. 80–82.

3. Bocharov is referring to the Parable of the Talents: Matthew 25:14–30. Cf. Luke 19:12–27.

4. A translation of this article into English appears in Bakhtin, *Art and Answerability*, pp. 1–2.

5. See Bakhtin, *Art and Answerability*, p. 1.

6. A translation of this fragment into English appears in Bakhtin, *Art and Answerability*, pp. 208–231.

7. Bakhtin, *Speech Genres and Other Late Essays*, p. 155.

TOWARD A PHILOSOPHY OF THE ACT

(S. Averintsev's notes are marked with asterisks; my additions to his notes are in brackets.)

1. Aesthetic activity is powerless to take hold of Being *insofar* as Being is an ongoing event, *insofar* as Being is in transit, in process of actual becoming. It is in this sense that Bakhtin speaks below of *sobytie bytiia*—"the ongoing event of Being," "Being-as-event," "Being-event" (cf. German *Seinsgeschehen*). Note Bakhtin's clarification in M. M. Bakhtin, *Art and Answerability* (Austin: University of Texas Press, 1990), p. 188 (footnote): "The *event* of being is a phenomenological concept, for being presents itself to a living consciousness as an [ongoing] event, and a living consciousness actively orients itself and lives in it as in an [ongoing] event." Cf. also Wilhelm Windelband, *An Introduction to Philosophy*, tr. Joseph McCabe (New York: Henry Holt, 1921; German edition 1914), p. 121: "In ontic questions the thing or substance is the central point; in genetic questions it is the category which is best called 'the event' [*Geschehen*]. This is the general expression for the Greek *gignesthai* [cf. Latin *fieri*]. This antithesis of the thing and the event is better than the earlier antithesis of being [*Sein*] and becoming [*Werden*]; for 'becoming' is only one aspect of the process of happening [*Geschehen*], which means, not only that something appears which was not there previously, but also that something which was there previously ceases to exist."

"Moment": Bakhtin's preferred term for a constituent of a dynamic whole. In this translation I render it either as "moment" or as "constituent moment." On wholes and moments, see Edmund Husserl, *Logical Investi-*

gations, tr. J. N. Findlay, 2 vols. (London: Routledge and Kegan Paul, 1970), vol. 2, investigation 3, chap. 2.

2. The meaning or sense (German *Sinn*) of the product of aesthetic activity is not that of a being in process of actual becoming; the product comes to be a participant in actual Being-as-event (that is, it is actualized or incarnated) through the mediation of our acts of effectual aesthetic intuiting.

"Enters into communion with": an attempt to render *pri-obshchit'sia*—to become a participant, sharer, partaker in (something) in common with (others), to become an active part of, to be incorporated into (as an active participant).

"Historical act": performed at one particular time and in one particular place by one particular individual. In this sense, "historical" is related to one of Bakhtin's key terms, *edinstvennyi*, which I render either as "once-occurrent" (German *einmalig*) or as "unique," "singular," "the only one," "the one and only" (German *einzig*). Cf. Heinrich Rickert's concept of "the historical" as that which is individual (in the sense of that which is qualitatively once-occurrent) in his *Limits of Concept Formation in Natural Science*, abridged ed., tr. and ed. Guy Oakes (Cambridge: Cambridge University Press, 1986), p. 78: "the historical in its most comprehensive sense" coincides with "the unique, invariably individual, and empirically real event itself."

3. "Images or configurations": the Russian *obraz* here is related to the German *Bild* in the sense of *Gebilde*, a produced formation.

"They do not partake in it": they do not participate in, are not part of, actual once-occurrent becoming (that is, they are not actualities in Being-as-event).

4. "Historical description-exposition": an alternative for "exposition" would be "representation" (of history). Cf. German *Darstellung*, and Rickert, *Limits of Concept Formation*, pp. 66–68.

"Fundamental split": "fundamental" for the Russian equivalent of the German *prinzipiell* and the French *principiel* (relating to that on which anything is ultimately founded or by which anything is ultimately regulated), one of Bakhtin's most frequently used terms. I render it for the most part as "essential and fundamental" ("essentially and fundamentally"), but occasionally also as "in its very principle," "in principle."

"Content or sense": for *soderzhanie-smysl*. I render this term below as "content/sense."

"Act/activity": for *akt-deiatel'nost'*—a given activity as expressed in an act, an instance of that activity.

5. "Unique unity" or "once-occurrent unity."
"Ongoing": closer to the Russian would be "in process of being accomplished."

6. "Sense or meaning": I render *smysl* and its derivatives both as "sense" and as "meaning" (German *Sinn, sinnhaft, Sinngebung*). For an illuminating introduction to the various uses of the term "sense" or "meaning," see Richard Schaeffler, "Sinn," in *Handbuch philosophischer Grundbegriffe*, Studienausgabe (Munich: Kösel, 1974), vol. 5, pp. 1325–1341 (with bibliography). See also "Sinn, II," in Rudolf Eisler, *Wörterbuch der philosophischen Begriffe*, 4th ed. (Berlin: Mittler und Sohn, 1930), vol. 3, pp. 69–71; E. N. Trubetskoi, *Smysl zhizni* [The Meaning of Life] (Berlin: Slovo, 1922), pp. 9–11; Gustav Shpet, *Appearance and Sense*, tr. Thomas Nemeth (Dordrecht: Kluwer Academic Publishers, 1991)—see index under "sense" (Shpet's book appeared in Russian in 1914).

7. "Acts of our activity": our activity is actualized in particular acts.

8. "Actually lived and experienced": life that is being lived-experienced. Bakhtin's term for experience or experiencing is always *perezhivanie*, lived-experience (German *Erleben* or *Erlebnis*; cf. French *vécu*).

9. I have chosen "answerability" instead of "responsibility" in order to foreground the root sense of the term—answering; the point is to bring out that "responsibility" involves the performance of an existential dialogue. For an initial orientation, see A. R. Jonsen, "Responsibility," in *Westminster Dictionary of Christian Ethics* (Philadelphia: Westminster Press, 1986), pp. 545–549. Jonsen contends that two works in the late nineteenth century gave the term a central place in the lexicon of morality: F. H. Bradley's essay "The Vulgar Notion of Responsibility and Its Connection with the Theories of Freewill and Determinism" (1878) and Lucien Lévy-Bruhl's *L'Idée de responsabilité* (1883). See also W. Molinski, "Responsibility," in *Sacramentum Mundi*, 6 vols. (New York: Herder and Herder, 1967–1970), vol. 5, 320–322; A. S. Kaufman, "Responsibility, Moral and Legal," in *The Encyclopedia of Philosophy*, ed. Paul Edwards, 8 vols. in 4 (New York: Macmillan and Free Press, reprint edition 1972), vol. 7, pp. 183–88.

For brief but informative treatments in German, see (under "Verantwortung") K. E. Løgstrup, in *Die Religion in Geschichte und Gegenwart*, 3rd ed., 6 vols. (Tübingen: J. C. B. Mohr/Paul Siebeck, 1957–1962), vol. 6, cols. 1254–1256 (note that the 2nd ed. of this dictionary, which came out in 1927–1931, did not include an article on "Verantwortung"!); and R. Egenter, in *Lexikon für Theologie und Kirche*, 10 vols. (Freiburg: Herder, 1959–1965), vol. 10, cols. 669–670.

An excellent elucidation of "Verantwortung" is provided by J. Schwart-länder, in the *Handbuch philosophischer Grundbegriffe*, vol. 6, pp. 1577–1588. Schwartländer points out that responsibility more and more frequently became a theme of philosophizing after World War I and that it clearly took over the place until then occupied "im allgemeinen sittlichen Bewußtsein" by duty or obligation (*Pflicht*).

10. *Postupok* (dictionaries usually define it as "an action intentionally performed by someone"): an action or act that I myself choose to perform, "my own individually answerable act or deed." This is Bakhtin's fundamental term throughout; he uses the word in the singular, presumably in order to bring out the focus on its singularity or uniqueness, on its being *this* particular action and no other, performed (answerably or responsibly) by this particular individual at this particular time and in this particular place. Furthermore, the focus is on the performing of the act or deed, or on the act or deed as it is being performed, in opposition to the consideration of the act *post factum* (the act that *has been* performed).

Bakhtin also uses the verb *postupat'* (to act, to perform an act), which is obviously connected with the noun *postupok*; and he gives a new sense to the verbal noun *postuplenie* by referring it back to *postupok*: a single, continuous performing of individually answerable acts or deeds and, therefore, analogous to the single act or deed.

In this translation I render *postupok* as "an act or deed," "a/the performed act" or "a/the act performed," "a/the deed."

11. "Validity" (*znachimost'*) is used here as an equivalent of the German *Geltung, Gelten* (being valid, operative, in force or in effect; validity, operativeness, obtaining). Thus, *tsennostnaia znachimost'* (German *Wertgeltung*) is something that obtains, is in force, is operative as a value or the operativeness, validity, obtaining of a value. For an elucidation of the concept (being-valid in distinction to being), see W. M. Urban, *The Intelligible World* (New York: Macmillan, 1929), pp. 149ff., 153ff.; and Eisler, *Wörterbuch der philosophischen Begriffe*, vol. 1, pp. 495–499. Kant spoke of the validity (*Geltung*) of the categories and the synthetic judgments *a priori*, insofar as they contain the "grounds for the possibility of all experience." Following Kant, R. H. Lotze introduced the term into German philosophy as a fundamental concept, fundamental not only for philosophy, but also for the sciences and for all cognition in general. In order to distinguish the normative from the merely factual, the Neo-Kantians elaborated a whole philosophy of *Geltung*.

12. "*The ought*" (*dolzhenstvovanie*) is an equivalent of the German *Sollen* (introduced into philosophical terminology by Kant). Note that "the ought"

(*dolzhenstvovanie*) and "(I) must" (*dolzhen*) have the same root, just as the German *Sollen* and *soll* do. The ought as "that which ought to be" is contrasted to "what *is*." Generally, that which is set before the will as valid and thus functions as a call or enjoinment to action. Cf. Rudolf Eisler, *Wörterbuch*, vol. 3, p. 106: The ought (*Sollen*) "is the correlate of a will, an expression for that which is required or demanded from a will (another's or one's own)." On Kant's use of the term, cf. Lewis White Beck, *A Commentary on Kant's Critique of Practical Reason* (Chicago: University of Chicago Press, 1960), p. 72: "if a rational being regards his maxims as universal laws, as he does when he says that some action that he does is the kind of action that all men (or other rational beings) should do, it cannot be by virtue of the material of the maxim, which refers to the object or the purpose of the will. . . . Beside the material of the maxim, however, there is only its form. The form of the maxim as expressed in an imperative is 'ought,' just as the form of every theoretical proposition is some mode of 'is.' As form, it is independent of any specific desire, which constitutes the content of specific maxims. If we abstract from an imperative all content by virtue of which it is addressed to a person motivated by a specific subjective desire, we are left with only the form, the skeletal 'ought.'"

13. "Rickert's affirmation-negation": see *Bejahung-Verneinung* in Heinrich Rickert's once celebrated book *Der Gegenstand der Erkenntnis*, 6th ed. (Tübingen: Mohr/Paul Siebeck, 1928; 1st ed. 1892). Rickert contends that cognition is a true judgment, and a true judgment consists either of the affirmation of a value or of the negation (denial, rejection) of a disvalue. What is peculiar to judging, therefore, is that it represents an either/or comportment; the affirmation is only one side of a pair of opposites, which consists of affirmation *and* negation. True cognition, then, is not the depicturing (*Abbilden*) of a transcendent Being but the recognition or acknowledgment of a "transcendent Ought"—the acknowledgment of values *or* the condemnation of disvalues.

Heinrich Rickert (1863–1936) was the founder and leader, together with Wilhelm Windelband, of a highly influential school of Neo-Kantianism at the beginning of the twentieth century. The best concise introduction to his philosophy as a whole is still Eduard Spranger's "Rickerts System," *Logos* 12 (1923/24): 1. See also H.-L. Ollig, *Der Neukantianismus* (Stuttgart: J. B. Metzler, 1979), pp. 59–66 (Ollig's brief treatment is concerned with locating Rickert within Neo-Kantianism as a whole); Urban, *The Intelligible World*, pp. 109ff., 150ff. (discusses Rickert's key concepts); and Iso Kern, *Husserl und Kant* (The Hague: M. Nijhoff, 1964), part 2, section 2, ##34–37 (examines Husserl's reading of Rickert and, in doing so, clarifies Rickert's key concepts and positions). The literature on Rickert available in English and French focuses above all on his theory of historical cognition: F. M. Fling, *The Writing of History* (New Haven: Yale University Press, 1920); Maurice Mandelbaum, *The Problem of Historical Knowledge* (New York: Harper and Row, 1967; 1st ed. 1938), pp. 119–147; Raymond Aron, *La Philosophie critique de l'histoire* (Paris: Julliard, 1987; 1st ed. 1938), chap. 2; Alfred Stern, *Philosophy of History and the Problem of Value* (The Hague: Mouton, 1962), chap. 5; Guy Oakes, "Rickert's Theory of Historical Knowledge," in Rickert, *Limits of Concept Formation*, pp. vii–xxviii. For a discussion of Max Weber's assimilation of Rickert's philosophy, see, for example, H. H. Bruun, *Science, Values and Politics in Max Weber's Methodology* (Copenhagen: Munksgaard, 1972).

14. "Veridicality-in-itself": its being true in itself (*istinnost' v sebe*).

15. This is Rickert's contention. See note 13 above: Rickert, *Der Gegenstand*, chap. 3, section 9.

*16. The name of Edmund Husserl (1859–1938) comes up here in connection with a paraphrase (perfectly correct in its essentials) of one of Husserl's theses, according to which the obligatory striving after truth cannot be derived from epistemology (a few lines later Bakhtin argues that the obligation to be ethical cannot be derived from ethics). But the entire course of Bakhtin's thought as a whole is essentially close to Husserl's approach. Husserl's phenomenology is oriented toward the indivisible unity of "lived-experience" (*Erlebnis*) and the "intention" contained therein. Bakhtin's key-concepts ("event," "event-ness," "a performed action": *postupok*) are similar in this respect to Husserl's *Erlebnis*, the sense of which, as we know, is by no means psychological; these key concepts are different in that they distinctly accentuate the problem of responsibility, which does not appear in this form in Husserl's thought. In this respect, Bakhtin is a distinctly Russian thinker, who continues the tradition of Russian nineteenth-century culture. For his thought, Dostoevsky's *oeuvre* was not only an object, but also a source.

17. "Validities": anything that has validity, is in force, or obtains theoretically, scientifically, ethically, etc. See note 11 above.

18. See p. 22 (Russian, p. 98), where Bakhtin begins his analysis of formal and non-formal ethics (or content-ethics). Cf. also the quotation from Beck in note 12 above.

19. "Attitude of consciousness": "attitude" (*ustanovka*) in the sense of *Einstellung*. Note that Bakhtin leaves no room for misunderstanding: he will approach the matter *phenomenologically*.

*20. Bakhtin's thought constantly revolves around a problem which is, in essence, a moral problem, and that is why it is so important for him to settle accounts with an illusion that was characteristic for the consciousness of the intelligentsia—the illusion of absolute and self-sufficient ethics. This illusion proves to be an inexhaustible source of moral nihilism. Experience demonstrates that the domain of "ethics as such," of "pure ethics," is only a certain formal position, namely, that of "duty." "Non-dogmatic" or "presuppositionless" ethics, however, will not tell us what exactly constitutes the "matter" or content of such a position, that is, what exactly should ("ought") the *subiectum* of obligation (of the "ought") do and in relation to whom? Nor will it tell us something more abstract: on what the ought itself is based. Ethics is not only incapable of grounding the fact of the ought, but it is itself grounded by that fact, is totally dependent upon that fact. The absolutization of ethics is simply an attempt to renounce the medieval conception of natural law as a God-given "table of commandments" in human hearts, while at the same time preserving the secondary derivations of that conception, and even reinforcing them and extending them on account of the space cleared by the departure of that conception; but flowers that have been cut off from their roots do not live very long. Outside of the metaphysics of natural law, on the one hand, and a sufficiently real social "commitment," on the other, the principle of abstract ought or obligation has demonstrated a frightening perversity: there proved to be nothing in the mind to hinder it from conceiving the ought as the ought-to-be of the *absence* of any ought, as Nietzsche showed. Pertinacious abstract reasoning, straining to ground the phantom of a natural law deprived of its ontological roots, has shown its impotence in the face of Nietzsche's questions and the questions of the numerous advocates of Dostoevsky's "underground man": "you ought, because you ought, because you ought"—absolutized ethics is incapable of getting out from within the confines of a logical circle, and this is keenly felt by all "underground men." Any real motivation whatsoever will be extra-ethical. This intellectual experience is complemented by the experience of lived life: there is a paradox (known since the time of the New Testament critique of "Pharisaism") to the effect that a person who has chosen to be specifically and above all else ethical is not particularly good, not particularly kind and attractive, since at every step he or she is distracted from an authentically moral self-forgetting by egocentric self-complacency or by an equally egocentric self-reproach. Ethics, when it is reduced to itself, left to itself, becomes a desolated ethics, for the ethical principle is a mode of relating to values, and not a source of values.

21. "Self-activity" (literally, "activeness"): the active operation of the Ego, or (in Kantian terms) spontaneity. On our existence as self-acting beings and on our experience of our own spontaneous activity in Kant, see Beck, *A Commentary*, pp. 194–196. See also "Spontaneität," in Eisler, *Wörterbuch*, vol. 3, pp. 140–141.

22. "Form" (in Kant) is an *a priori* unity of ordering of a sensible manifold. See also Rickert, *Der Gegenstand*, pp. 139ff. (form and content in epistemology).

"Transcendent": in Kantian terms this should be "transcendental."

23. Kant's "Copernican achievement" or, more commonly, "Copernican revolution" in the theory of cognition: just as Copernicus asserted that the earth revolves round the sun, so Kant contends that to have knowledge of finite, empirical reality, this reality must conform to the structure of the human mind, and not the mind to the reality. Or, as Norman Kemp Smith puts it, "Objects must be viewed as conforming to human thought, not human thought to the independently real" (*A Commentary to Kant's "Critique of Pure Reason"*, 2nd ed. [New York: Humanities Press, 1962], p. 18; see also pp. 22–25, on misunderstandings of the analogy). The metaphor "Copernican revolution" goes back to a passage in the preface to the second edition of the *Critique of Pure Reason*: B xvi–xvii.

24. "A universal consciousness," etc.: all these are equivalents of the German terms *Bewußtsein überhaupt, wissenschaftliche Bewußtsein* (Hermann Cohen's term), *erkenntnistheoretisches Subjekt* (Rickert's term: see Rickert, *Der Gegenstand*, chap. 1, section 7). On *Bewußtsein überhaupt*, see Eisler, *Wörterbuch*, vol. 1.

25. "Act/deed of its actualization": the actual performance of its actualization.

26. "Fundamentally and essentially": *prinzipiell*; see note 4 above.

*27. "First philosophy" (Gr. *prote philosophia*)—Aristotle's term for fundamental ontology, which lays the foundations for all further philosophizing. See *Metaphysics* 4.1.1003a21: "There is a science which investigates being as being and the attributes which belong to this in virtue of its own nature"; 4.1.1026a32: "it will belong to [first philosophy] to consider being *qua* being—both what it is and the attributes which belong to it *qua* being" (*The Works of Aristotle*, translated into English under the editorship of J. A. Smith and W. D. Ross, 12 vols. [Oxford: Clarendon Press, 1908–1952], vol. 3). For a historical orientation on "first philosophy," see C. F. Gethmann, "Erste Philosophie," in *Historisches Wörterbuch der Philosophie*, 7 vols. to date (Basel/Stuttgart: Schwabe, 1971–), vol. 7, cols. 726–729.

28. The 1986 publication (p. 87) has a lacuna here: "[2 illegible words]." For the English translation, S. G. Bocharov has kindly provided the result of a new reading of the manuscript: *teoreticheskikh mezheverii*. The problem with this reading is the word *mezheverii* (the nominative singular would be *mezheverie*), which no one seems to know. Any attempt to translate it would be sheer guesswork.

29. *"Participative* thinking": *uchastnoe myshlenie* (this could be expressed in German as *teilnehmendes* as well as *anteilnehmendes Denken*)—engaged, committed, involved, concerned, or *interested* thinking; *unindifferent* thinking (I occasionally add "unindifferent" in parentheses after "participative"). For an example of how Bakhtin explicates "participative thinking," see p. 19, footnote (Russian, p. 96).

Bakhtin's expression may be related to the German *das seinsverbundene Denken*, which S. Marck, for example, defines as thinking that derives from or relates to "eine reale Existenz" (an actually existing human being); the position of *seinsverbundenes Denken* expresses the contention against the *Bewußtsein überhaupt*, against the logical construction of the pure cognizing *subiectum*. See S. Marck, "Zum Problem des 'seinsverbundenen Denkens,'" *Archiv für systematische Philosophie und Soziologie* 33 (1929): 238–252. It might also be relevant to recall here Kierkegaard's term "interest." See, for example, H. M. Schmidinger, *Das Problem des Interesses und die Philosophie Sören Kierkegaards* (Freiburg/Munich: Karl Alber, 1983), chap. 9, sections 4–7. Cf. also P. F. Strawson's distinction between the "participant" and the "detached" standpoints from which human behavior may be viewed, in his *Skepticism and Naturalism* (New York: Columbia University Press, 1985), pp. 33–36: the standpoint of participation and involvement is the standpoint that we naturally occupy as social beings committed to participant relationships and acting under the sense of freedom, and it constitutes an understanding of objects or events that involves sharing or sympathizing with. See also Douglas Browning's commentary on Strawson's distinction in his *Ontology and the Practical Arena* (University Park: Pennsylvania State University Press, 1990), chap. 1.

30. Ontological proof of (or argument for) the existence of God: the existence of God follows necessarily from the concept of God. See "ontologisches Argument," in Eisler, *Wörterbuch*, vol. 2, pp. 346–349. In his refutation of the ontological argument Kant uses the example of a hundred real thalers in distinction to a hundred conceived (possible) thalers: "A hundred real thalers do not contain the least coin more than a hundred possible thalers. For as the latter signify the concept, and the former the object and the

positing of the object, should the former contain more than the latter, my concept would not, in that case, express the whole object, and would not therefore be an adequate concept of it" (*Critique of Pure Reason*, tr. Norman Kemp Smith [New York: St Martin's Press, 1965], A 599/B 627 [p. 505]). See Heinz Heimsoeth's commentary in his *Transzendentale Dialektik* (Berlin: W. de Gruyter, 1969), part 3, pp. 474–486.

For analyses of Kant's refutation, see S. L. Frank, *Predmet znaniia* [Object of Knowing] (Petrograd: Istoriko-filologicheskii fakul'tet Imp. Petrogradskogo Universiteta, 1915), pp. 162–168; Martin Heidegger, *The Basic Problems of Phenomenology*, tr. Albert Hofstadter, rev. ed. (Bloomington and Indianapolis: Indiana University Press, 1988), part 1, chap. 1 (Kant's Thesis: Being is not a real predicate); Georg Picht, *Kants Religionsphilosophie* (Stuttgart: Klett-Cotta, 1985), pp. 460–461, 469–470; A. W. Wood, in *The Cambridge Companion to Kant*, ed. Paul Guyer (Cambridge: Cambridge University Press, 1992), pp. 397–401; and Dieter Heinrich, *Der ontologische Gottesbeweis: Sein Problem und seine Geschichte in der Neuzeit* (Tübingen: J. C. B. Mohr, 1960).

31. "Valuative" (for *tsennostnyi*): expressive of value. Alternatives: axiological, value-governed, value-related (cf. German *werthaft*).

*32. Strictly speaking, Bakhtin's citation is inexact; what is important for Kant is that ten "real" thalers are not greater than ten thalers in my mind—that their reality adds nothing to their numerical sum (since Anselm proceeded from the opposite—the real is "greater" than what exists only in the mind, and, therefore, the concept of the greatest includes reality as one of its perfections).

33. "Fundamentally and essentially": *prinzipiell*; see note 4 above.

34. "As projected" (*v zadanii*): in the mode of a task to be accomplished or of something to be determined.

35. "Fundamentally": *prinzipiell*; see note 4 above.

36. "Essentially and fundamentally": *prinzipiell*; see note 4 above.

37. "Eternal": it always is what it is, it is not subject to any temporal determination, it is timeless. Cf. Shpet, *Appearance and Sense*, p. 33.

38. "What-is-to-be-attained": *zadannost'* as opposed to *dannost'*. Equivalents of German *Aufgegebenheit* as opposed to *Gegebenheit* (deriving from *aufgegeben* and *gegeben*): the latter means "something given, what-is-given" (in the sense of a concretum) or (in the sense of status) "givenness"; the former, "something given as a task-yet-to-be-accomplished" or "a problem-yet-to-be-solved" or "a concept-yet-to-be-determined," as well as "givenness in the mode of a task (yet-to-be-accomplished)." Besides "what-is-to-be-

attained," I also use such phrases as "something-yet-to-be-achieved" or "yet-to-be-accomplished" or "yet-to-be-determined." Cf. Rickert on the category of "givenness or factuality" in *Der Gegenstand*, chap. 5, section 3.

"Penitent tone": expressing the sense of one's own deficiency, inadequacy, failure.

*39. What Bakhtin means to say (and he is entirely justified in doing so) is that Plato's teaching, in opposing the immutability of "the truly existent" and the mutability of what only seems to have being (the *me-on*), does not aim at all at a simple constatation of the difference between ontological levels, but aims at orienting human beings in relation to these levels: what is expected of a human being is an active choice—i.e., in Bakhtinian terms, an answerable act or deed [*postupok*], or, in other words, a human being ought to flee what only seems and seek to attain what is true.

*40. One should recall here Husserl's constant struggle against psychologism, which he reveals, for example, in the work of nineteenth-century positivists. [See "Psychologismus," in the *Historisches Wörterbuch der Philosophie*, vol. 7, cols. 1675–1678; Eisler, *Wörterbuch*, vol. 2, pp. 550–555; Martin Heidegger, *Die Lehre vom Urteil im Psychologismus* (Leipzig: J. A. Barth, 1914), in his *Frühe Schriften* (Frankfurt/Main: V. Klostermann, 1978), section 5, pp. 161–164; Marvin Farber, *The Foundation of Phenomenology* (Cambridge: Harvard University Press, 1943), chap. 4; Herbert Spiegelberg, *The Phenomenological Movement*, 2 vols. (The Hague: M. Nihjoff, 1960), vol. 1, pp. 93–95. Cf. Rickert's characterization of psychologism in *Der Gegenstand*, p. ix: psychologism believes that on the basis of a doctrine about a *part* of the Real it is possible to form the concept of the *whole* of the theoretical world.]

41. "Participatively": as in "participative thinking"; see note 29 above.

42. "Participative-effective experiencing": for "participative," see note 29 above.

43. *Lebensphilosophie* (philosophy of life): a designation common in German histories of philosophy for a philosophical trend that arose around 1900. Its chief representative in France is Henri Bergson. In Germany it is represented by Wilhelm Dilthey as well as Georg Simmel, Rudolf Eucken, and Ernst Troeltsch. In Rudolf Eisler's definition: "that trend in philosophy which defines the absolute reality (*Wirklichkeit*) as 'Life' or which opposes irrational living reality, which can be grasped only through lived-experience (*Erlebnis*) or through intuition, to that mode of Being which has been formed by intellectual-analytic and abstractive cognition" (Eisler, *Wörterbuch*, vol. 2, p. 16). It should be stressed that the expression "philosophy of

life" in this sense characterizes the whole of philosophy, and not a particular branch of philosophy.

*44. Henri Bergson (1859–1941): The most conspicuous philosophical sensation and even philosophical *aventure*, as it were, at the beginning of the twentieth century. Bergson's power of attraction was to a considerable extent due to the fact that one sought and found a new type of philosophizing in his works, a type of philosophizing (unthinkable for the materialism and positivism of the nineteenth century) which integrated moments of the soul's immediate experience in an incomparably more comprehensive way than anyone had done since the time of Schelling. It is characteristic that Bergson exerted an influence on the poets of his time, first and foremost on Charles Péguy, but also on Paul Valéry. [A. E. Pilkington deals with Bergson's influence on Péguy, Valéry, Proust, and Julien Benda in his *Bergson and His Influence* (Cambridge: Cambridge University Press, 1976). On Bergson as a "philosophical sensation," see R. C. Grogin, *The Bergsonian Controversy in France 1900–1914* (Calgary, Alberta/Canada: University of Calgary Press, 1988), and *The Crisis in Modernism: Bergson and the Vitalist Controversy*, ed. F. Burwick and P. Douglass (Cambridge: Cambridge University Press, 1992), which includes a translation by Charles Byrd of Bakhtin's "Contemporary Vitalism," pp. 76–97.]

45. N. O. Losskii, *Intuitivnaia filosofiia Bergsona* [The Intuitive Philosophy of Bergson] (Moscow: Put', 1914; there were two editions in 1914, and a third edition came out in 1922: Petersburg: Uchitel', 1922). See also Roman Ingarden, "Intuition und Intellekt bei Henri Bergson," *Jahrbuch für Philosophie und phänomenologische Forschung* 5 (1922): 285–461; Josef König, *Der Begriff der Intuition* (Halle/Saale: M. Niemeyer, 1926), section 2, chap. 5; and Martin Buber, "Zu Bergsons Begriff der Intuition," in his *Werke*, 3 vols. (Munich: Kösel; Heidelberg: Lambert Schneider, 1962–1964), vol. 1, pp. 1073–1078. Intuition is fundamental in N. O. Losskii's own philosophy: see his *The Intuitive Basis of Knowledge*, tr. Nathalie A. Duddington (London: Macmillan, 1919), a translation of Losskii's *Obosnovanie intuitivizma*, which had three editions—in 1906, 1908, and 1924; a German translation by J. Strauch appeared in 1908 (Halle/Saale: M. Niemeyer) as *Die Grundlegung des Intuitivismus*.

46. "Participative thinking": see note 29 above.

47. "Essentially necessary": *prinzipiell*; see note 4 above.

48. "Essential and fundamental": *prinzipiell*; see note 4 above.

49. "Confession": in the sense of an accounting to oneself for one's life. See Bakhtin, *Art and Answerability*, pp. 143–149.

50. "Empathizing": for a critical analysis of empathy, see Bakhtin, *Art and Answerability*, pp. 61ff. Empathizing, according to Bakhtin, is a necessary but insufficient act in aesthetic contemplation as a whole. In the present text Bakhtin uses a synonym for empathizing, *vzhivanie*, which is equivalent to the German *Sich-Einleben*.

51. "Transgredient": see Bakhtin, *Art and Answerability*, note 11 (p. 233).

52. "A *subiectum* situated outside the bounds of that life": see Bakhtin, *Art and Answerability*, p. 14 and note 28.

*53. Bakhtin means Schopenhauer's reflections on the perception of music in the third book of Schopenhauer's *The World as Will and Representation*, and also chapter 39 ("On the Metaphysics of Music") in the supplements to the third book. [For a comparison of Schopenhauer's aesthetics and Th. Lipps's theory of empathy in art, see O. Schuster in *Archiv für Geschichte der Philosophie* 25 (1912): 104–116. On Schopenhauer's treatment of music and on aesthetic contemplation, see Ulrich Pothast, *Die eigentlich metaphysische Tätigkeit* (Frankfurt/Main: Suhrkamp, 1982), pp. 98–107 and 48–51, 88, 250–255; and also Julian Young, *Willing and Unwilling: A Study in the Philosophy of Arthur Schopenhauer* (Dordrecht: M. Nijhoff, 1987), chap. 7 (in aesthetic consciousness we "lose" ourselves entirely in the object of perception so that we are no longer able to separate the perceiver from the perception).]

54. S. G. Bocharov was kind enough to inform me that the efforts to develop a coherent reading of this passage have yielded the following inconclusive result (possible variant readings are placed in brackets): "*Velikii simvol aktivnosti*, niskhozhdenie [samootdanie?] Khristovo—*v prichastii, v* raspredelenii [?] *ploti i krovi ego preterpevaia permanentnuiu* [*permanentno?*] *smert'*, *zhiv* [*zhivo?*] *i deistvenen* [*deistvenno?*] *v mire sobytii, ego ne-sushchestvovaniem v mire my zhivy* i prichastny [prichastiem?] emu, ukrepliaemy." Italicized words seem to be less uncertain than others.

55. "Event-ness": insofar as Being is an ongoing event; see note 1 above.

56. Compared to the Russian text published in 1986, this is a new reading of the first 5 lines on p. 95 in the 1986 publication. I would like to express my gratitude to S. G. Bocharov for making this new reading available for the English translation.

57. "Essential and fundamental": *prinzipiell*; see note 4 above.

58. "Think participatively": the footnote provides a definition of "participative (unindifferent, engaged) thinking"; see note 29 above.

*59. This critical characterization of Neo-Kantianism is exceptionally apt. It should be enough to recall the direction in which Ernst Cassirer's thought developed more and more distinctly. [Cf. Shpet's highly critical comments on Neo-Kantianism in his *Appearance and Sense*, pp. 13, 123–124.]

60. "First philosophy": see note 27 above.

61. "Defects and defaults" for *nedostatki i nedochëty* (*nedochëty* implies a failure in required execution or procedure). This qualifying phrase was omitted in the 1986 publication; I am grateful to S. G. Bocharov for making it available for this translation.

62. "Participative consciousness": an engaged, unindifferent consciousness; see note 29 above.

63. ["Illegitimate substitutions? faults?"] (*podmeny? nedochëty?*): one word is illegible here, and the words suggested are purely conjectural. "Incongruities" for *nesoobraznosti*: the Russian word is actually more negative (cf. German *Ungereimtheiten*).

64. "Theosophy," "anthroposophy": for brief introductions, see the *New Catholic Encyclopedia*, 15 vols. (New York: McGraw-Hill, 1967), vols. 1 and 14. See also "Anthroposophie," "Mystik, mystisch," and "Okkultismus," in the *Historisches Wörterbuch der Philosophie*, and "Anthroposophie" and "Theosophie," in *Die Religion in Geschichte und Gegenwart*.

65. The passage from "In the present context" to the end of the paragraph was deleted in the 1986 publication. Again, I have to thank S. G. Bocharov for making it available for this translation. The deleted Russian text reads as follows: "My zdes' mozhem ostavit' v storone vopros o tom, putëm kakikh [podmen? nedochëtov?] i metodicheskikh nesoobraznostei sovershaet istoricheskii materializm svoi vykhod iz samogo otvlechënnogo teoreticheskogo mira v zhivoi mir otvetstvennogo istoricheskogo sversheniia-postupka, dlia nas vazhno, odnako, chto etot vykhod im sovershaetsia, i v etom ego sila, prichina ego uspekha. Drugie ishchut filosofskogo udovletvoreniia v teosofii, antroposofii i pod. ucheniiakh, vpitavshikh v sebia mnogo deistvitel'noi mudrosti uchastnogo myshleniia srednikh vekov i Vostoka, no kak edinaia kontseptsiia, a ne prosto svodka otdel'nykh prozrenii uchastnogo myshleniia vekov, sovershenno neudovletvoritel'nykh i greshashchikh tem zhe metodologicheskim porokom, chto i istoricheskii materializm: metodicheskim nerazlicheniem dannogo i zadannogo, bytiia i dolzhenstvovaniia." For an example of an extended critique of historical materialism in Russian, see P. I. Novgorodtsev, *Ob obshchestvennom ideale*, part 1 (4th ed., Berlin: Slovo, 1922), chap. 2. See also Hermann Cohen's critical comments on the "materialistic view of history" in his *Ethik des reinen Willens*, 3rd ed. (Berlin: B. Cassirer, 1922), pp. 39f., 315.

66. "Being-event of life": the being of life insofar as that being is an ongoing event; see note 1 above.

67. "Essentially and fundamentally": *prinzipiell*; see note 4 above.

68. "Altruism," "Cohen's ethics": For a historical orientation on altruism, see "Altruismus," in *Historisches Wörterbuch der Philosophie*, vol. 1, cols. 200–201. For a helpful exposition of Hermann Cohen's ethics, see Walter Kinkel, *Hermann Cohen: Eine Einführung in sein Werk* (Stuttgart: Strecker und Schröder, 1924), pp. 164–245. See also Eggert Winter's historical and systematic study of Cohen's conception of ethics: *Ethik und Rechtswissenschaft* (Berlin: Duncker und Humblot, 1980).

69. "Content-ethics and formal ethics": Bakhtin uses here Russian equivalents of the German expressions *materiale* and *formale Ethik*; I use an alternative of the former—ethics of content (i.e., matter in contrast to form). On the contrast of "material" ("matter") and "form" in Kant's ethics, see, for example, Beck, *A Commentary*, pp. 96, 134. Generally, an ethics of "form" specifies the motives of conduct, while an ethics of "matter" ("material") specifies the objective content of an action or its ends.

70. "Fundamental and essential": *prinzipiell*; see note 4 above.

71. "Universal": *obshchii*, like the German *allgemein*, that is, "applicable to all," as Bakhtin says in the preceding sentence. Alternatives: "common to all" (pertaining equally to all in question) or "general" (pertaining to all persons belonging to a category).

72. "Inadequate thinking": closer to the Russian *ne-do-myslie* would be "failure to reach the level of thinking in the full sense of the word."

73. "Free volition": a rendering of *vole-iz-volenie* (*not* the familiar *vole-iz-iavlenie*, "an expression of the will," like the German *Willensäußerung*). *Vole-iz-volenie* comes closest to the Latin *liberum voluntatis arbitrium* (free choice of the will). Chr. Wolff translated *arbitrium* into German as *Willkür* (the will's complete freedom of choice); Kant used *Willkür* in the sense of the power to act or omit to act as one pleases. Cf. Latin *liberum arbitrium*, freedom of action, the power to decide as one pleases (*ad arbitrium*).

74. "Fundamentally and essentially": *prinzipiell*; see note 4 above.

*75. It is characteristic that ethical conduct is motivated, as in the Gospels, by personal love of the one who gave the commandments: "If ye love me, keep my commandments" (John 14:15).

76. "Universality": like the German *Allgemeinheit* (generality); see note 71 above.

77. There were 3 illegible words in this passage in the 1986 publication. S. G. Bocharov provided the following new reading: "gde obychno prois-

khodit sniatie[?] vsekh printsipov i privnesenie . . ." Possible alternatives for the word read as *sniatie* are *smena, otmena*.

78. "'Material' content": see note 69 above.

79. "Compellentness": *nuditel'nost'*. This term could also be translated as "compellingness." I have chosen "compellentness" in order to convey something of the uncommonness of the word *nuditel'nost'* in modern Russian (in contrast to the familiar *pri-nuditel'nost'*, compulsoriness, being necessitated by force). E. V. Volkova, *Estetika M. M. Bakhtina* [M. M. Bakhtin's Aesthetics] (Moscow: Znanie, 1990), p. 14, points out that the term "compellent" or "compelling" (*nuditel'no*) denotes an ought or obligation which issues from an individual's inner conviction, as opposed to an imposed or enforced obligation (expressed by *pri-nuditel'no*).

80. "Categoricalness": unconditionality.

81. "Categorical imperative": an unconditional (as opposed to a condi tional or "hypothetical") imperative. On Kant's "categorical imperative," see H. J. Paton, *The Categorical Imperative* (Chicago: University of Chicago Press, 1948), pp. 113ff., 129ff.

82. "Non-contingent" or non-fortuitous, not a matter of chance.

83. "Universality": see note 71 above.

84. Again, Bocharov provides an amended reading of lines 8 through 11 (up to the period) on p. 101 in the 1986 publication: instead of *spravedlivosti* read *opravdannosti*, and the rest of the sentence now is "i imenno v etoi svoei teoreticheskoi opravdannosti lezhit zakonnost'[?] kategoricheskogo imperativa kak obshchego i obshche-znachimogo."

"Theoretical justification": literally, "justifiedness" (its being justified theoretically).

85. "Act only on that maxim through which you can at the same time will that it should become a universal law"; "Act as if the maxim of your action were to become through your will a Universal Law of Nature"; "So act that your will can regard itself at the same time as making universal law through its maxim." Quoted in Paton, *The Categorical Imperative*, p. 129. A "maxim" is a principle actually at work in our action, i.e., the real ground of our act.

86. "Into communion with": actualizing it in a historical act or performance of cognition and thus of acknowledgment; see note 2 above.

87. "Philosophy of culture": *Kulturphilosophie* as used in German historical classifications of philosophies. It characterizes the whole of a philosophy, and not a branch of philosophy. For example, Rickert's philosophy as a whole could be characterized as a philosophy of human culture in its totality. See also Bakhtin, *Art and Answerability*, note 141 (p. 249).

88. "The unique truth [*pravda*]": Bakhtin uses two words to denote "truth": *pravda* (derived from "right," "just," or "true-to") and *istina* (derived from "is"). Note that in this sentence he already marks the specific sense of truth as *pravda*: "the *unique* truth of *both* the fact and the sense in their *concrete unity*." He clarifies the contrast between *pravda* and *istina* on p. 46 (Russian, p. 110). Cf. in this connection, Martin Heidegger's distinctions at the beginning of his lecture on metaphysics: *Was ist Metaphysik?* (Frankfurt a. M.: V. Klostermann, 1975), pp. 24ff.

89. "Hypothetical": conditional.

90. "Psychologism": see references in note 40 above.

91. "Something-to-be-achieved" (German *Aufgegebenheit, Aufgegebenes*): given in the mode of a task-to-be-yet-accomplished; see note 38 above.

92. "Elemental and blind": "blind" is literally "dark," and "elemental" may have the connotation of "anarchic." Cf. German *elementar und dunkel*.

93. "Ongoing event": the event in process of being accomplished.

94. "As something given and as something-to-be-achieved": *gegeben/ aufgegeben—dany i zadany* (German *gegeben/aufgegeben*), that is, *both* are present at the same time, conjointly; see note 38 above.

95. "Palpable-expressive": "palpable" (*nagliadno*) as an equivalent of the German *anschaulich*.

96. "Fundamentally and essentially": *prinzipiell*; see note 4 above.

97. Note that Bakhtin expressly proposes a phenomenological description.

98. "Participatively": see note 29 above.

99. On the concept of "world," see L. Landgrebe, "The World as a Phenomenological Problem," *Philosophy and Phenomenological Research* 1 (1940–1941): 38–58; J. J. Kockelmans, *The World in Science and Philosophy* (Milwaukee: Bruce, 1969), pp. 55–72; J. N. Mohanty, "Thoughts on the Concept of 'World,'" in *Essays in Memory of Aron Gurwitsch*, ed. Lester Embree (Washington, D.C.: Center for Advanced Research in Phenomenology and University Press of America, 1984), pp. 241–247; Michael Gelven, *A Commentary on Heidegger's Being and Time*. rev. ed. (DeKalb: Northern Illinois University Press, 1989), pp. 47–68; and R. Bernet, "Husserl's Concept of the World," in *Crises in Continental Philosophy*, ed. A. B. Dallery and C. E. Scott with P. H. Roberts (Albany: State University of New York Press, 1990), pp. 3–21.

100. "In conjunction with another given": "something given" in the sense of being "totally present-on-hand" (*vorhanden*) and "something given in the

mode of a task" (*aufgegeben*). The point to note is that both "givens" are present in conjunction, inseparably.

101. "Palpable (intuitable)": a rendering of the Russian equivalent of the German *anschaulich*.

102. "Valuative": expressive of value, value-governed, value-related. Cf. German *werthaft*.

103. For a fair exposition of Rickert's theory of values, see W. H. Werkmeister, *Historical Spectrum of Value Theories*, 2 vols. (Lincoln, Neb.: Johnsen Publishing Company, 1970), vol. 1, chap. 9.

104. See Rickert, *Der Gegenstand*, pp. 193–195: "There exist real *objects* which, as one says, *possess* value. A work of art, for example, is an object-reality of this kind. But the value that it possesses, or the value that attaches to it, is clearly not identical with its reality: everything real about it (canvas, paints, etc.) does not belong to the value it possesses. Object-realities linked with values we shall call, therefore, *goods* [*Güter*], in order to differentiate them from the values attaching to them. Furthermore, values must also be strictly separated, at least conceptually, from the psychic acts of valuation performed by a real *subiectum*, and indeed from any real valuation. It is certainly true that for us values are always conjoined with actual valuations or that we can *find* values only in actual goods. But since values are conjoined *with* the realities, they are not the same as the actual valuations or the actual goods."

105. "Philosophy of culture": *Kulturphilosophie*; see note 87 above.

106. What follows below is an explication of modern *Kulturphilosophie*.

107. Thomas Hobbes, *Leviathan*, chaps. 17 and 18.

108. See note 88 above.

109. "Fundamental and essential": *prinzipiell*, principled; see note 4 above.

110. "I, too, *exist* . . . in the whole": *et ego sum*—I am, and therefore . . . That is, I myself exist (in the emphatic sense of the verb) as well—together with all others.

111. "*My non-alibi in Being*": Bakhtin's formulation could be explicated as follows: I cannot be relieved of answerability for the commission of an act by an *alibi*, that is, by claiming to have been *elsewhere* than at the place of commission.

112. "Come to know of and to cognize": *uznavat'/poznavat'*. The difference is between knowing something (identifying it) and coming to a full cognition of it. Cf. German *kennen/erkennen*.

113. "I universalize it": or, alternatively, I generalize it. See note 71 above.

114. "Irreplaceability": there is no substitute for it, one cannot substitute something else (another action) for it.

115. "Actor": doer, agent.

116. What follows below presents the ways in which my passivity and my self-activity manifest themselves in a distinct yet undivided form. The numbers have been added by the translator.

117. "*Must* actualize": the Russian word for "must" (*dolzhen*) has the same root as "the ought" (*dolzhenstvovanie*).

118. See note 10 above (*postupok*).

119. "My fellow-being" [*moi blizhnii*]: the Russian word here relates to the New Testament "neighbor," as in "love thy neighbor."

120. "Obligatively unique": unique as it ought-to-be.

121. "Contingent possibility": fortuitous or chance possibility.

122. "Universal": general; see note 71 above.

123. "Given and projected": both as something given (totally on hand) *and* (simultaneously) given in the mode of something yet to be determined.

124. "Obligative": ought-to-be.

125. "Participative self": a *subiectum* who participates in an engaged, interested manner; see note 29 above.

126. "A detached (non-participating) consciousness": an unengaged, impersonal consciousness.

127. "Fundamentally and essentially": *prinzipiell*; see note 4 above.

128. "My intimate": someone very close to me, related to me (such as a family member).

129. *Znanie/uznanie*: again a play on knowing or knowledge similar to the German pair *kennen/erkennen*.

130. *Pravda*: see note 88 above.

*131. What Bakhtin has in mind here are the highly characteristic anti-Platonic and anti-Christian motifs in Nietzsche—the motifs of exalting "life" as appearance and illusion in opposition to the repudiated "true world" of invisible and immutable spiritual being. Nietzsche's last word is precisely this illusion of life, consciously grasped and accepted in full *as* illusion. The concept of "eternal returning" is opposed to the modern European conception of progress. "Life" is absolutized as a fundamental and essential absence of meaning that provokes, in and by itself, orgiastic ecstasy; hence the image of the Greek god of orgies—Dionysus. In Russia, the "Dionysian" aspect of Nietzsche's doctrine was popularized by Viacheslav Ivanov, although Ivanov noticeably reduced Nietzsche's nihilistic aspiration and aggressive drive.

[On *Dionysiertum* in Germany, see Martin Vogel, *Apollinisch und Dionysisch* (Regensburg: Gustav Bosse, 1966), pp. 247–280, esp. 259–261; R. Hinton Thomas, *Nietzsche in German Politics and Society 1890–1918* (Manchester: Manchester University Press, 1983).]

132. The passage following "The unbridled play of empty objectivity" was marked as illegible ("[15 illegible words]") in the 1986 publication of the Russian text (p. 120). The passage was subsequently deciphered, and thanks to Bocharov's kindness, I can include it in the English translation. In Russian, the deciphered passage reads as follows: "sposobna lish' poteriat' vsiu nalichnuiu bezyskhodno-nuditel'nuiu deistvitel'nost', no sama pridaët lish' vozmozhnuiu tsennost' [?] beskonechnym vozmozhnostiam."

133. "Loving[?] corporeality[?]": the incarnated (flesh-and-blood) human being.

134. In Bakhtin's manuscript, this text is interpolated in parentheses after "all theoretical possible knowledge of the world"; it was omitted in the 1986 publication of the Russian text. Thanks to Bocharov, I am including it in the English translation in the form of a footnote. The passage in Russian reads as follows: "(dazhe fakt, tol'ko teoreticheski poznannyi, kak fakt est' pustaia vozmozhnost', no ves' smysl[?] suzhdeniia imenno v tom, chto ono obyknovenno ne ostaëtsia teoreticheskim suzhdeniem, a deistvitel'no priobshchaetsia edinstvennomu bytiiu, zdes' trudno vsiakoe otvlechenie ot svoei deistvitel'noi prichastnosti)."

135. This is an amended reading, provided by Bocharov, of the sentence in the first two lines of p. 122 in the 1986 publication. The Russian is as follows: "i samo eto bol'shoe tseloe slozheno ne iz obshchikh, a konkretno-individual'nykh momentov."

136. This clause is a translation of the amended reading provided by Bocharov: "i iznutri ego produkta, i s tochki zreniia avtora . . ."

137. See the brief characterization of Dante's "map of the world" in Bakhtin, *Art and Answerability*, p. 208.

138. "State of civilization": in Spenglerian terms, the state following the end of a living, developing culture. On the *Kultur-Zivilisation* antithesis in German, see *Europäische Schlüsselwörter*, vol. 3: *Kultur und Zivilisation* (Munich: Max Hueber, 1967), pp. 288–427 (Michael Pflaum), esp. pp. 338ff. (Highpoint of the Antithesis: Oswald Spengler).

139. For Russian philosophical responses to Tolstoyism, see P. I. Novgorodtsev, *Ob obshchestvennom ideale*, 5th ed. (Berlin: Slovo, 1922), pp. 125–137; N. A. Berdiaev, "Dukhi russkoi revoliutsii," in *Iz glubiny* (Paris: YMCA-Press, 1967), pp. 95–102; I. A. Il'in, *O soprotivlenii zlu siloiu* (London,

Canada: Zaria, 1975; reprint of the 1925 Berlin edition with a supplement by N. P. Poltoratskii).

140. On Oswald Spengler (1880–1936), see W. H. Dray, in *The Encyclopedia of Philosophy*, vol. 7, 527–530. For a contemporary response, see the collection of articles by S. L. Frank, F. A. Stepun, N. A. Berdiaev, and Ia. M. Bukshpan: *Osval'd Shpengler i Zakat Evropy* (Moscow: Bereg, 1922). See also S. Averintsev's article on Spengler's "morphology or culture," in *Voprosy Literatury* 1 (1968): 132–153.

141. "Consciously comprehended": can become an object of full awareness, something consciously grasped in full.

142. "Participative": see note 29 above.

143. "Is a necessary," etc.: "neobkhodimyi, no ne ischerpyvaiushchii moment moei deistvitel'noi dlia menia tsentral'nosti." Bocharov has provided this phrase as a reading of the passage that remained undeciphered in the 1986 publication (second line on p. 125).

144. "Intuitable-palpable": "palpable" (*nagliadnyi*) as an equivalent of the German *anschaulich* (the opposite of conceptual or abstract).

145. "Eternal": see note 37 above.

146. "*This* actuality of a consciousness and *this* actuality of a book" refers to "*this* actual, once-occurrent thought" and "*this* actual book" at the end of the preceding paragraph.

147. See the preceding note.

148. See the discussion of the time and space of a human life in Bakhtin, *Art and Answerability*, pp. 208–209.

149. "Event-relations": not only relations between events, but also relations that have the character of ongoing events.

150. "Architectonic structure": instead of the Latinism *structure* Bakhtin uses the Russian equivalent of it—*stroenie*, "structure" or "construction." Note that the structure or organization of the world-as-event is characterized as "architectonic," that is, the structure of the world-as-event results from the architectonic interrelationship.

151. Bakhtin paraphrases a Russian proverb here: *Ne pó khoroshu mil, a pó milu khorosh*, "he is dear to me [I love him] not because he is good, but he is good because he is dear to me."

152. "Event-architectonic": the architectonic has the character of an event.

153. On "objective aesthetic love," see Bakhtin, *Art and Answerability*, pp. 81–83, 90.

154. On the correlation with mortal life, see Bakhtin, *Art and Answerability*, pp. 101–112.

155. This clause is a translation of the new reading provided by Bocharov that differs from the 1986 publication (line 14 on p. 131): "Unichtozhim moment zhizni smertnogo cheloveka . . ."

*156. Cf. Psalm 90.10: "The days of our years are threescore and ten."

157. "Parting"—*Razluka*: "Dlia beregov otchizny dal'noi . . ." (written on November 27, 1830, in Boldino). In the ms. the poem has no title; it was published posthumously (in V. A. Vladislavlev's *Utrenniaia Zaria* for 1841) under the title "Parting." The poem is in memory of Amalia Riznich, one of Pushkin's loves in Odessa. She was the daughter of an Austrian banker; her mother was Italian. In May 1824, she left Odessa for Italy and died of consumption in Genoa in May 1825. See the similar analysis of this poem in Bakhtin, *Art and Answerability*, pp. 211–221. Neither analysis is intended as an exhaustive treatment of the artistic whole: both single out only those moments of the whole which are pertinent in each context. In *Art and Answerability* Bakhtin is concerned with showing with a specific example how the concrete human being as the center of values functions within an artistic whole. The purpose of the analysis in the present volume is, as Bakhtin explains, to give a preliminary idea of the possibility of a concrete, value-governed architectonic, the architectonic of the world of the performed act, by way of an analysis (with a concrete example) of the architectonic of the world of aesthetic seeing, since this latter world shares certain features with the world of the answerable deed.

158. *Vne-nakhodimost'*: being outside or situatedness outside the bounds of; see note 52 above.

159. Not only the spatial-temporal context of her life, but also the context of values that her life constitutes.

160. "Concretized *qua* event": it has the character of an ongoing event. Cf. in the next sentence "accomplished as an event."

161. "Valuatively consolidates": "consolidates" for "gives body (bodily consistency) to." This consolidating is governed by or charged with values.

162. On "horizon" and "environment," see Bakhtin, *Art and Answerability*, pp. 97–99.

163. "Event-moments": those moments of the context which have the character of ongoing events.

164. "Event-meaning": the meaning of the world of Italy as an ongoing event.

165. Bocharov has provided a new reading of this clause (p. 134 in the 1986 publication): "no v etom tone ikh uzhe predvoskhishchaetsia . . ."

166. "Event-moments": the moments of Being-as-event, hence the moments themselves have the character of events.

167. "The experiencing of Italy as event," that is: the experiencing has the character of an ongoing event.

168. "Event-context": not just context of events, but a context that itself is an ongoing event.

169. "Event-relation": a relation that is an ongoing event.

170. "Event-eternity": the events want to continue as events independently of any temporal determinations.

171. "To refer an object to the valuative plane of the *other*": see Bakhtin, *Art and Answerability*, pp. 134, 189.

172. "This architectonic is something-*given* as well as something-*to-be-accomplished*": see note 38 above.

173. "Self-exclusion": or exclusion of self, self-exception. The new reading provided by Bocharov is *sebia-iskliuchenie*.

174. Clearly, Bakhtin is not satisfied with Hermann Cohen's logical construction of the Other in his *Ethik des reinen Willens*, pp. 209–215 (on p. 213 Cohen proposes the Other as a concept that is more precise than *Nebenmensch*). For a contemporary Russian critique of Cohen's ethics, see Evgenii Trubetskoi, "Panmetodizm v etike" [Pan-Methodicalness in Ethics], *Voprosy Filosofii i Psikhologii* 20:2 (97) (March–April 1909): 121–164. See also Cohen's *Die Religion der Vernunft aus den Quellen des Judentums* (Leipzig: Gustav Fock, 1919), chap. 8 (The Discovery of Man as Fellow-Man), and P. Probst, "Mitmensch," in *Historisches Wörterbuch der Philosophie*, vol. 5, cols. 1416–1419. For an initial orientation on the problems of the relationship of I and the Other (I and Thou), see the following: Michael Theunissen's articles in the *Historisches Wörterbuch der Philosophie* on "der Andere" (vol. 1), "Du" (vol. 2), "Ich-Du-Verhältnis" (vol. 4), as well as his article on the "Ich-Du-Verhältnis" in *Die Religion in Geschichte und Gegenwart*, vol. 3, and his book (translated by Christopher Macann) *The Other: Studies in the Social Ontology of Husserl, Heidegger, Sartre, and Buber* (Cambridge: MIT Press, 1984); J. Hinrichs, "Dialog, dialogisch," in *Historisches Wörterbuch der Philosophie*, vol. 2; A. Halder/H. Vorgrimler, "Ich-Du-Beziehung," *Lexikon für Theologie und Kirche*, vol. 5, pp. 595–598; S. L. Frank, *The Unknowable*, tr. B. Jakim (Athens: Ohio University Press, 1983; the Russian original, *Nepostizhimoe*, appeared in 1939), chap. 6 (Transcending Outward: The "I-Thou" Relation).

INDEX

THEME INDEX